THE HANDBOOK OF THE
NAVIGATOR

T7

THE HANDBOOK OF THE

NAVIGATOR

By Eric J. Pepin

Edited by Christopher E. Robison

Compiled by Eric T. Robison

Higher Balance Publishing
Portland, Oregon

T7

Higher Balance Publishing
515 NW Saltzman Road #726
Portland, Oregon 97229

Phone: 1-800-935-4007
Fax: 503-626-8157
Email: publishing@higherbalance.com
Web: www.higherbalance.com

Book and cover design: Matt Struve

FIRST EDITION

Library of Congress Control Number: 2004108835

The Handbook of the Navigator / Eric J. Pepin

ISBN 0-9759080-0-6

"All that is gold does not glitter,

not all those who wander are lost.

The old that is strong does not wither,

deep roots are not reached by the frost.

From the ashes a fire shall be woken,

a light from the shadows shall spring.

Renewed shall be blade that was broken,

the crownless again shall be king."

- J.R.R. Tolkien

CONTENTS

CONTENTS

CONTENTS

PREFACE

There are experiences in life that mere words cannot express. The only way to truly understand them is to directly experience them for yourself.

This book is not an ordinary book. It is an extraordinary mechanism to recreate within you, the reader, a very special effect. It creates a vibration of specific thought that I call multi-dimensional consciousness. This is achieved by a series of thought patterns or what I call realizations. I first discovered this process when I was very young and it has had a powerful effect on my life as I am sure it will on yours.

I was about seven years old on a warm summer day. The air was laced with the scent of dry grass fields and the hum of buzzing insects in the distance. I was sitting on the steps to my home listening deeply to the melody of sounds and the smells of nature. The harmony of scent and sound gave way to great inner peace for me and it still does to this day.

This harmony moved my consciousness to a place in my mind I was unfamiliar with but it felt completely natural. I now refer to this place as 'the in-between'. Within that place I felt something directing me ever-so subtly to walk out into a nearby field that was overgrown with tall dry grass.

I found a small path and began to walk towards the center of the field, knowing somehow that it was my destination. I knew there was a small pond in the field, once used for dairy cows. I had ice-skated on it with friends during the winter months but had not returned since the spring.

On my way down the path I became aware of grasshoppers that were resting on dried blades of grass. Stopping for a moment I looked at one and it seemed to look back at me. I remember a stillness and quietness came over me. I was unaware of anything happening around me as I was drawn into the grasshopper. My eyesight had become clearer and enhanced but it did not seem to completely be my eyesight. I was aware of the firm structure and color of the grasshopper with its legs holding the stem of the grass and its mouth moving slowly and then rapidly. Its eyes seemed to

almost speak to me. I had merged and become one with the
grasshopper.

Then I suddenly inhaled. I had forgotten to breathe for a moment.
During my inward breath I detached my mind from the
grasshopper and continued my walk towards the pond in the center
of the field.

The harmonious sounds of that day again filled my ears as
summer's warmth wrapped around me. There seemed to be
nothing but the field and the buzzing sounds of nature all around
me. I felt a deep sense of peace and calm.

I knew somehow that something was about to be revealed to me
and it was important to allow myself to experience what was
happening.

The path widened and gave way to a shimmering golden pond with
the sun reflected on its surface. As I walked closer I noticed the
smell of the field became blended with the scent of water and mud.
They became new instruments in the harmony of scent and sound
for me that afternoon.

The shimmering pond beckoned my young and curious mind.
After spotting a large stone outstretched from the embankment into
the water, I decided to lie down. Lying down on the stone, facing
the water, I began to experience the sun's warmth contained in the
rock. It embraced me and I openly accepted its warmth.

I noticed my reflection in the pond and moved to a better position. The sun and small moving clouds behind my image gave me a sense that I was looking at someone other than myself. Then something moved underneath the surface of the water and caught my eye. As I was peering through the glassy water that was separating my reflection to what was hidden behind it, I noticed an underwater micro world.

Hundreds of frog eggs were clinging to the pond's weeds. A myriad of water insects were spiraling and swimming around. The frog eggs drew me in and I noticed it was as if they were a galaxy of life unto themselves, with new life contained within each majestic orb. Then the summer sunlight penetrated the water in golden beams and separated the shadows of darkness.

Once again, I had almost forgotten to breathe so I took a deep breath inward. I rolled over onto my back and looked up into the blue sky while soaking up the sun's warmth. I became aware of a distant buzz slowly growing louder and louder. In fact, it grew so loud it alarmed me. Just before I leapt to my feet, a dragonfly flew within inches of my face. My entire being was exhilarated with a rush of adrenaline as it quickly sped away along with the alarming buzz it seemingly created.

Standing, I looked at the field around me. I took a deep breath and felt myself filled with an internal hum. It was a blissful vibration as if the dragonfly's buzz was now within me but I could not detect exactly from where.

It rapidly grew more intense and enveloped my entire being. It pulsated through me. At that moment, I became aware of every cell in my body humming in harmony with the others. I then felt compelled to look up into the sky. I watched as the bright blue sky gave way to patches of night sky until the daytime had quickly become night!

Suddenly in the middle of that summer day, stars appeared, and much like how I experienced the grasshopper, they seemingly became larger within themselves. I was aware of their presence both visually and internally.

The stars were moving through me.

I breathed in deeply and they quickly faded away into the blue sunny sky. The internal humming faded and I felt a great peace within me.

I slowly looked in a circular motion all around me taking notice of the pond, the field, the insects, the birds, and the forest trees.

I realized that all is one.

It was at that very moment that something surfaced within me. It was a memory that seemed to add to my being; a missing piece of who or what I was. I recognized that something had guided me to experience that moment and that I had chosen unknowingly to listen to it. I now listen to it everyday of my life and have come to call it the Navigator.

May the Navigator be awakened within you and may it guide you to what you have been seeking your entire life; completion.

Eric Pepin

*Your whole life has been a search for meaning,
purpose, and completeness.*

*You are aware of a sense within you that seemingly directs you
as if it were a compass navigating your essence.*

*This navigator gives you a sense of knowing; directing you
away from the trappings of mans religions and structured
thinking.*

It is elusive to structural thinking.

*An in-between place that defies logic
as humanity understands it.*

*Your hidden senses tell you, that what your eyes see,
and hands touch, is not all that there is.*

*You look around in a distant way and then you listen deeply,
breathe deeply, feel deeply and*

*It is then that you know that there is a veil between you and
some other place that holds an understanding
to that which you are.*

*Then, without seemingly knowing, you want, and need,
to become one with IT.*

Do you remember?

CHAPTER ONE

THE NAVIGATOR

THE NAVIGATOR

Your whole life has been a search for meaning, purpose and completeness.

I know you. We have met before. It is likely that you will think this is not true and cannot be possible. You may feel a comfortable certainty in the fact that I cannot know you, as we have never met.

If you could ask me what your name was, could I tell you? Or where you were born, where you live and what you do? No, I could not answer these things. I do not know the name given to you, nor where you were born, or what paths and places you have wandered during your life.

Yet, I say again; I know you.

I would go so far to say that I know you better than you know yourself. It is not the person reading this book that I am familiar with. I know the forgotten part of you that yearns for knowledge which will lead to peace and completion. I know what lies within you and what it is trying to help you do.

I have been searching for you for so long. All of my life I have been preparing for this moment. The moment we finally meet and I can say to you, at long last, welcome Navigator. I have so much to share with you. It is time to begin.

It is time for you to awaken.

THE DESIRE OF THE SEEKER

I am about to share with you what the Navigator is. However, I must also tell you that it is not something that is easily described. It is elusive but it holds a profound secret that, once realized, will change your life forever.

I am going to humbly compare you to a salmon. I want you to think about the journey of a salmon. Now, I know it does not have a consciousness as you do and that it cannot think as you do. The salmon has much to share with you if you will but compare it to your own journey and open yourself to see the truth.

Imagine you live in a vast ocean. All of your life, as long as you can remember, you have lived in this great water world, teeming with life. You see, a salmon is born far from the ocean in fresh water rivers. It travels down into the sea and reaches maturity there only to journey back to its hatching grounds before it dies.

You probably remember very little from early childhood. Had you traveled down a river when you were very young most of what you would remember would only be of the world where you grew up.

As a salmon, your first memories are of this huge ocean. It is a brilliant and beautiful world. There are so many things to experience and places to see. This ocean world is so large and filled with so many places to see one could wander for lifetimes and never even consider the possibility of anything outside of it.

You, of course, are different.

All of your life you have lived in this great ocean of life. When you were younger, you enjoyed life in the ocean and all it had to offer. However, somewhere in the back of your mind you always felt there was something more somehow beyond it. There was a feeling, deep inside of you, that made you restless. It made you think that the world you knew and loved was somehow keeping you from discovering a place beyond it all that held an answer to the very essence of your being. This feeling made you yearn for something you could not see with your eyes but believed existed. All of your life this feeling has spoken to you, it has made you question the world around you. You have always tried to push this feeling aside, discounting and questioning any purpose in acting on it.

Still, this feeling always remained within you.

Then on a warm day with the sweet spring current sweeping in from the south, something happened. You were going about your life and everything was normal. Then it was as if something flipped a switch inside of you. The strange feeling you had always felt welled up and it was as if everything in your body spoke with a single, undeniable voice.

You have a purpose.

It was as if some instinctual part, something deep within you, was screaming to be heard. It was greater than any hunger you had ever known. Any thirst or emotional longing had never compared to this need. This feeling, this instinctual call, does not have a specific name or design. It is not a blueprint or map.

A salmon would not have the intellect to consider these things but even if it did, do you think it would understand? At some point a salmon's instinct tells it to return. If it did have our intellect it would probably try to rationalize what it was feeling and why. It would repress this feeling.

Have you felt something similar that you have tried to ignore? If so, then you can see how your journey and the journey of this imaginary salmon are beginning to relate.

Being beyond your ability to understand, you tried to repress this feeling as well. You are just a simple salmon, how could you have a special purpose? You tried to shake it off but the feeling would not leave you. Nobody else you knew seemed to fully understand.

It was much like the old yearning you had always felt but so much stronger. Still, it made no sense. There was no explanation for it. Worse yet, the questions grew stronger and your longing grew greater. It continued to speak to you.

You are more than what you seem.

Desperate, you began to try and find answers in those around you. The other fish could not relate to this strange desire that lived within you. Not giving up so easily you began searching the stories of others. They were ancient texts and their truths uncertain, yet they spoke of a place beyond the ocean. These texts spoke of brave souls who journeyed far beyond the confines of the ocean and came back to help others find their way. These stories gave you some comfort and you tried to use them to quiet your inner gnawing.

It did not take long for the restlessness to return. The feeling inside instinctually felt right but it fought against every rational thought you had. Still, the feeling would not be satisfied. It offered no relief but to hear its cry.

Return.

You can question no more. Your strange instinct fills you with an uncertain desire and drives you to seek this unknown place.

Against all odds, you begin your journey of discovery. It begins as all journeys do, with a single step, a simple moment of choice. It is a daunting task, with an uncertain goal. The world is boundless. The chances of finding this hidden place are almost impossible. Everything is set against you finding your way. Still, you feel you cannot help but try, fighting against every rational thought that suggests your search is in vain.

Think about how amazing it is that a salmon, with very little intelligence at all, will travel from an enormous ocean and find the one river it was born in. Out of all of the other streams and rivers pouring into this huge ocean it searches for one specific channel and finds it. It is lucky for the salmon it does not consider the odds of fulfilling its task. Given similar odds most people might not even begin.

This is one important lesson you can gain from your life as this humble salmon. Despite the reflection of doubt and uncertainty that we have given it for this story, it chooses to listen to its instinct. It puts effort into an earnest search. Now, let us continue your journey as a salmon.

For a long time you swim through the ocean. For a long time you search trying to follow this all-consuming instinct, going far beyond the place you began.

Then one day you happen to swim upon a small, bubbling cove. Within the cove a current of water pushes from above, plunging you to the floor and filling the little cove with bubbles. Thick, brilliant green moss lines the walls. It is a strangely familiar place, one you had visited many times when you were very young.

While our salmon can only see this bubbling cove we can conceive that it is a small waterfall where a stream meets the ocean. It is only perspective. It does not understand something we see as obvious.

Now consider that there are many things in your life that you do not understand because you lack a higher perspective. Humbly speaking, one of the reasons I chose the salmon is that in many ways, we are as small and simple on our journey to awakening as the fish is back to its own source. Keep this idea of perspective in mind as we continue to follow your life as a salmon back to its source.

Weariness sets in and you slide to the floor feeling defeated. It seemed as if you had traveled so far, only to end up back where you began. In anger, part of you immediately wants to get up and swim far away from this cove and redouble your efforts to continue your quest. Another part whispers quietly to lie down, rest and take a breath. This whisper moves you to feel like letting go, which to you, feels like defeat. You quickly resist this idea until you notice this whispering part is that same old feeling, deep inside, that seemed to urge you down this path so long ago.

Exhausted and beaten you give in and accept this quiet feeling and lie down. It is then you notice a strange feeling in the current splashing down from above. Curious, you swim closer. For a moment you feel the water moving through the current is somehow different. Then you shake it off and quickly decide there is nothing there at all. Yet, it gives you a sense of inner stillness and after a pause you decide the water is indeed strange and that it must be followed. You take a moment to look back at the great ocean, the world you know. The current will take you beyond the familiar world you can relate to and following it means you will be moving against the flow.

Then, without thinking or expecting much, you push to follow it. It is difficult at first as the current pushing against you is strong and nothing like the world you lived in before. It takes a great deal of effort. Every gain you make is threatened by the fear that if you stopped the current would suddenly push you right back to where you began.

Suddenly a giant shape crashes into the water from above. It is brown with swirling fur and long, sharp spikes that resemble teeth. Unprepared for such an event you pause only to be suddenly pushed back by the stream! Fearful of losing ground you push awkwardly as the brown claw smashes into your side. You scream in shock and tighten up as the claw pulls you from the water! Then everything moves in slow motion and a feeling of incredible calm surges through your being. It urges you to relax, let go, and surrender. You listen to it as you, very gently, twist your body. Naturally, your body slips out of the claw. As you begin to fall you feel as if the world has stopped.

You look around and see the great, silvery stream shining in the sun. Except you are above it! You see it in a way you had never imagined before. It climbs far ahead of you with many other streams branching off and merging into one. Looking back you can also see it winding down into the great ocean where you came from.

Your mouth opens in awe as you realize it is all connected. The ocean where you began, the stream you have been swimming through and the very place you are seeking. This knowledge somehow empowers you and opens your mind as you begin to see a larger picture beyond just your lone search.

Your own spiritual journey will also have many obstacles and dangers.

The danger for you, as with the salmon, is that you will not make it to your destination. There is a purpose the salmon is trying to fulfill in reaching the source. Your own journey is not so different.

Often, in the process of struggling and overcoming the obstacles in your path, you have profound realizations and experiences. The salmon was attacked by the bear and lifted from the water. On one hand, you could say its life was in danger. On the other hand, you could say it released its fear and overcame the bear. Even more, the experience altered the salmon's perspective and allowed it to see and realize something it never would have had been able to otherwise. Fear is the mind-killer. Of all the obstacles through life, it is fear that often poses the greatest danger. It can prevent you from continuing on your way. Luckily, you are a brave salmon, and surviving the bear only empowers and strengthens you.

Your body hits the water and you drop into a swirling pool, back into the world.

There you see other fish and almost instinctively you know; they are like you, they know what you are seeking. Searching you find that many currents lead away from the pools but only one leads to the source. Knowing there are others who are seeking with you gives you a sense of comfort. Still, none seem to know the way and you consider that your search may be in vain. As before, it seems when you begin to accept defeat and surrender, your instincts rise to be heard.

You have a purpose that is calling to you. There are many obstacles on your journey and many dangers that await you. Against the greatest of odds, this purpose must be fulfilled.

Determined to fulfill it you search the pool until you find a current that has the strange water that seems to call to you. It is also moving through the strongest current crashing down from above. Thinking, you tell yourself it cannot be right, that you must find an easier path. Another part in you instinctually leaps out and you feel compelled to push up the fiercest stream.

Struck with amazement at how long you follow the stream you begin to question the sense in following such a thing. It seems illogical that you should work so hard to follow something that might not lead anywhere or serve any reasonable purpose.

This is the problem with your intellect, it allows you to understand but it causes you to question. It causes you to doubt the very instinct within you. Many times you cannot even tell if the strange water is real or just a figment of your imagination. It does not look any different, or smell different; in fact, none of your senses seem to suggest there is anything different about it at all!

Your instinct does not exist outside of you in the physical world so your brain tried to explain it by creating something it could understand. In this case it led you to believe there was something elusive and different about the water. You were able to accept this and follow it until you realized what it truly was. It is more of a feeling, than anything, which tells you to keep following it. It is your deep, inner instinct, calling and directing you to the source where you began. Even though you recognize it, that does not mean you will not continue to question following it. With every passing moment struggling against the current, you fill with an increasing desire to abandon your chosen route.

Suddenly you push out of the strong current into a large quiet pool, the likes of which you have never seen before. Giant crystals, glistening and shining with brilliant colors protrude from the sides of the pool. Refracted light bounces and plays across everything.

The entire pool radiates with a deep, cool current and an air of mystical beauty.

Wonder so fills your entire being that you have trouble breathing and cannot help but choke back tears of joy. Before, where your heart was troubled with doubt it now beats with renewed spirit and vigor. For a time you pause and much of you longs to remain in this place. It gives you hope and instills in you a sense of mystery about the world you have never felt. This experience, this discovery, fills you with encouragement to keep following your strange instinct despite the lack of any certainty that it will ever lead you to the place you seek. With a purposeful thrust, you continue on your way.

Your journey is long.

Many times, frustrated, uncertain and weary, you abandon your search. At these times you live quietly in the calm pools. Each time your memories of the crystal pool, and other amazing discoveries you found along your search, stirs you to continue on your journey. Your strange inner instinct leads you to new places, unique places, different from anything you have seen before. Each discovery pushes you onward with renewed vigor and intensity.

In time, you cease questioning where your instinct will take you. You learn to trust it, even through the darkest of waters that are devoid of any light. Stranger still, you begin to sense that it is not taking you away into the unknown, but bringing you back to a place you have always known.

Whether by chance or some design of fate, when at last you cease questioning it, you push into a deep, dark pool whose bottom you cannot see. You can feel no current coming from any direction. Fear and shock begin to overwhelm you as you consider that it is a dead-end. You have failed. It is time to give up.

You are weary and while you fear defeat and ultimately your death, you accept it.

It is then the familiar feeling deep inside of you stirs slightly. Having learned through your long journey to trust this feeling, you take a deep breath and release your fears. Then, you quiet your thoughts and listen intently, trying to become aware of everything around and within you. It is then this feeling inside of you grows stronger and you have a sudden urge to look up.

All of this time you have been slowly sinking and you are floating near the bottom. You see shining flashes of silver, other salmon, strange and ethereal in appearance are there with you. Shining golden globes line the floor and you are filled with a feeling of great peace and joy.

You have reached the source. It is here that a part of you will die yet another part of you will be reborn.

Your own journey will not appear the same. It will not be finished in a small pool with other fish and fish eggs lining the riverbed floor. It will be similar in that it is the moment all of your instincts are driving you towards. Attaining that moment will give you peace beyond description. It will give you completion. If you were a salmon, do you think you would feel so very different?

BEFORE THE NAVIGATOR CAN BE FOLLOWED, IT MUST BE FOUND

The Navigator is like the salmon's instinct. It can help you find a path among the experiences in your life and will lead, at last, into an awakened state of consciousness. This state will allow you to experience your higher consciousness. While you may not realize it now this awakened state is everything you have been searching for, it is completeness. It will not be as simple as finding a stream, but if followed, the Navigator will lead you to awaken into your higher consciousness.

You may wonder why I call it an awakened state of consciousness. Are you not already awake? The truth is, you are in a sleep. Not an ordinary restful nighttime slumber, this sleep is very different and far from ordinary. It has clouded your senses and turned your world into a dream.

Just like a normal dream, part of you knows that you are asleep, that you are dreaming. This part of you, this sense within you, is trying to help you wake. If the pull of intuition, of instinct, is strong, if you seek to discover the truth of existence, know that this pull, this desire, is the 'Navigator'.

It is difficult to follow something that you do not recognize. In the journey up the stream the feeling deep inside was always there, trying to lead you. It pushed you to begin your search. However, it was not until you stopped and recognized it was something within you that you began to truly follow it. That was the moment of recognition. That is when you realized the feeling was more than a feeling, it was a separate thing. It was the Navigator.

To follow the Navigator you must first recognize and acknowledge it exists.

Like the strange instinct leading through the winding streams, you should follow where the Navigator leads. Much like a compass, the Navigator directs your essence. However, also like a compass, the Navigator can only be a helpful guide. It is still up to you to follow it.

This is not as easy as it sounds.

A compass is a tool you can touch and hold in your hands. In our physical material world, seeing is often believing, which is not how the Navigator works. It is a hidden sense. It tells you there is more to this world than what your eyes see and hands touch. There is something beyond this life and there is a reason for this existence. The guiding pull of the Navigator feels like an instinct. The path set by the Navigator leads to a revelation that will unveil the truth of your being.

THE TRUTH OF YOUR BEING

You have known your entire life that you are here to serve a greater purpose. What you do not know is exactly what that purpose is or what the driving force behind it is. Yet, ever since you were young, you have been aware of it.

Realizing that sense of purpose, feeling it, is the first moment the Navigator makes itself known to you. In its own way your Navigator is trying to reveal to you the nature of your being. How much it reveals to you depends on the choices you make.

For the Navigator to be effective we must listen to it, because like any other instinct, we can repress it, ignore it or be strengthened by it. The Navigator provides an instinctual sense of the truth. As babies, instinctually we know to suckle milk from our mother, so too instinctually we know that the Navigator leads to knowledge that will aid in awakening. This instinct alone will not lead to awakening. You must refine your ability to understand what the Navigator is saying.

It is the responsibility of individuals to train themselves to listen and be aware of the Navigator's communications. Even if it is ignored and pushed away, the Navigator can never be destroyed.

In the journey up the stream, there were many times the instinct was ignored or abandoned. Yet, the instinct was still there, waiting for you to listen to it and continue on your journey. The Navigator is a part of you, waiting for you to recognize it and choose to listen, so that it can fulfill its purpose and help you achieve your higher purpose.

That is right, you have a higher purpose.

Although you may have already felt this throughout your entire life, it is important to acknowledge it. As I mentioned earlier, feeling is the first way the Navigator begins to subtly reveal itself. Are you beginning to see the quiet way of the Navigator? Its purpose, its very design, is to help you achieve yours.

Your higher purpose ties strongly into what you really are. Beyond who you are right now, the person reading this book, there is another part of you. It is your higher self. It is your higher consciousness.

Our higher consciousness is the truest form of what we are. It is the culmination of all of our lives and experiences. I said lives because we are capable of moving beyond the life we are living now and being reborn into another. Our higher consciousness may contain the memories of a great many lives, or this life may be our first. The higher consciousness is really our soul, which is just another word to describe it. It is our most complete consciousness.

Imagine if every time we read a book we forgot everything else about our life, or any other book we have ever read and believed we were the character in the book. It is an absurd thought but that is what has happened!

We have forgotten the totality of what we are. We believe we are only our immediate personality, living this one life in this one body at this one time. That is what it means to be asleep. We have forgotten all that we are. The Navigator is trying to reach down and show us we are not the person in the book but the one reading it with knowledge far beyond the simple pages of our life!

MASTER THE ART OF LISTENING

Of course, it is easier to *say* we are more than what we are, than it is to *know* we are more than what we are. The very nature of our higher consciousness makes it difficult because it is so alien to how we often believe reality works.

Our higher consciousness does not exist in our brain; it exists in a separate place, a dimensional place. Our higher consciousness is trying to get information to us, who we are right now, from this other place. This is why we were instilled with the Navigator, so that part of our higher consciousness could be here to relay messages.

We often interpret this communication only as an intense driving desire to connect to something beyond our moments in life. It so fills our being that its push is as powerful as our desire to live. It is every fiber of our soul fighting and screaming to live.

The Navigator is trying to ensure our higher consciousness's existence.

It knows that we are aging and it knows that we will leave this life at some point. It is fighting for our survival. It is fighting for us to find what it is we need to complete our being.

It is very similar with the salmon. Its body or biological clock knows, on some level, its life expectancy is running out. Every instinct in its being is fighting one last battle for it to reach its final destination and fulfill its purpose. It is a natural instinctive process for the salmon to return to the place it was born and create new life.

We have a similar instinctual urging.

While this push is not for us to return to the place of our physical birth and procreate, as is the purpose of the salmon's instinct, it is to ensure the survival of a form of life on a different level. It is the Navigator fighting to ensure the survival of our higher consciousness and it has a limited amount of time to do it. The odds are against it as we have poisons in the air, fatty foods, disease and war. It retains everything forming in our minds, determining how we are going to exist when we leave this planet and how far we will go and what our existence will be.

There is a driving need for us to connect and discover spiritual knowledge that goes beyond just an interest or a curiosity. This need is our Navigator struggling to find a way to help us awaken to our higher consciousness. It is the survival instinct of our higher consciousness.

This process is difficult because we cannot understand the meaning of the message from our higher consciousness with normal human thinking. The way the brain thinks is too structured and the knowledge of our higher consciousness is without constructs!

At this stage, we receive bits of information and the Navigator helps us find tools and knowledge that we add to our brain to help it develop and interpret the message of our higher consciousness, which will lead to awakening. This is the purpose of the Navigator and what it is really trying to do. It is trying to find the knowledge, the tools, the equipment or the wiring for what we are building! We are building a receiver to download our higher consciousness into our current consciousness.

The Navigator knows what we need and it will tell us, "use this part, do not use that one, and throw this away! This knowledge or technique is good stuff, but this other stuff is bad!" The Navigator is trying to help us build a better translator so we can receive messages from our higher consciousness. This is why the Navigator, unable to work directly within the confines of the brain, seeks out other senses to help us translate these messages.

In the salmon story, the strange instinct, which is the Navigator, helped you to navigate through the winding streams. It helped you choose which path to take and urged you to keep going. In life, it is very similar. It is a guide that tells us what experience, or knowledge, is right for us, and what is not.

The difficulty is in knowing what it is really saying.

Remember it is like an instinct so it communicates internally. That communication will not be like a voice inside your head yelling, "Hey John! We need to talk!" or, "Hey Mary you better listen up I got something to say!" It will not be a booming voice, calling out your name and commanding you to follow its instructions.

What about animals that migrate, how do they know when to migrate and where to go? Do you think if you were a salmon you would hear a salmon voice in your head telling you what to do? Do animals hear voices that go, 'Moo, moo', or, 'meow, meow, bark, bark, howl'? Do birds hear an internal squawking that tells them when to fly south? No. It will be a quiet inner knowing. This inner knowing does not have a word or a name for it. This knowing is similar to the inner knowing that a pregnant woman might experience when she craves unusual foods for the vitamins or minerals that her body needs.

When people experience a feeling, or a sense of knowing something they might otherwise not know, it is often associated with intuition. Intuition is the way in which the Navigator manifests itself. In that way, you can look at intuition as a tool of communication. It is your higher consciousness trying to get past the brain so that it can deliver its message.

MOVING BEYOND IS LEARNING TO TRUST

Imagine an airplane sitting on a runway. For the sake of this analogy, let us say that the ground is our brain. Our whole life we yearn to fly, to know the highest regions that call to us from the bright blue sky. The sky is our higher consciousness. We spend most of our life on the ground, in our head.

Even though we like it on the ground, moving on the ground is very different from how we could move flying through the air. Because we yearn to fly we know the only way to experience what it is really like to fly is to do it.

For us to achieve flight we need to know where we are going and how to get into the air. That is why we have our trusty pilot, the Navigator. The Navigator tells us to sit back, relax, have a pillow and close our eyes. The Navigator tells us to take a deep breath and to not fear leaving the ground, which has held us our entire life. Of course, a pilot is no good unless they have a plane to carry us where we want to go. This is why we also have a plane called Intuition.

Now we are ready.

We have to trust our pilot, the Navigator, and the plane, Intuition, which will take us into the sky. The Navigator uses the vehicle, Intuition, to pick up momentum, and it needs a lot of momentum. The plane engines are powerful but they need quite a bit of runway time and speed running those wheels because the brain will not let us take off so easily, it wants us to believe we cannot ever leave the ground.

With Intuition, the Navigator can get us there. We can blast down the runway and then when we have enough speed, lift off into the sky, our higher consciousness.

In order for the airplane to successfully take off it must first gain lots of speed as it goes down the runway. Only after it has enough speed can it lift into the air, and take flight. Intuition is like the airplane running down the runway and we must use it until eventually it goes beyond the brain and starts to lift off the pavement of just a physical level and goes into impossibilities we could never get from rational deduction.

Intuition for most people is partially the sixth sense and partially logical deduction based on experience. It is bridging two ways of thinking like the plane bridges the ground and the sky by moving between them. If our experience in this physical life does not rationally deduce how we would know something intuitively or in any other way then we know there is something more to it. It is a matter of reaching the point where we move beyond just using our brain. The Navigator is trying to help us find that momentum.

This momentum is trying to help us listen to our higher consciousness and learning how not to think with our brain. The brain is in conflict with the higher consciousness. They are in conflict because messages from the higher consciousness will not fit in our brain. These messages are like square pegs that we are trying to force into circular holes.

Our brains are very selective about what we can receive and they naturally reduce the bountiful amount of information that waits in the higher consciousness. We must go through the process of teaching our brains to think differently. This process will be difficult because when we use our brain, it sets up conduits and structures that dictate the methods by which we process data.

In time, our brain takes these conduits and structures and uses them to filter data automatically without our knowing. We set up the process and it follows our programming. As we awaken, we must learn to relax the structures of the brain and develop a clear consciousness to remove the filters and ease this information through.

As the constructs of the brain loosen it also refines how clearly the Navigator can be felt. Remember the long journey up the stream? At the very end, you were overwhelmed with terror, when you believed you had simply reached a dead-end. It was at that final moment, when the greatest discovery was closest, you thought of giving up. It was only because you had learned to trust your Navigator that you found what you were looking for. You ignored rational thought and used another kind of knowing.

If you want to connect to your higher consciousness and awaken, you must begin to trust enough to leave the ground.

As the plane pushed into the sky, you must push into the dimensional place where your higher consciousness exists. Not only does your higher consciousness carry memories of your previous lives but also knowledge from existing as a dimensional being.

You cannot be fully aware of your dimensional self because your complete being exists in a kind of coma.

This is another way of looking at what it means to be asleep. You still function in a limited sense as any human does but your full and total knowledge of being is waiting to harmonize with your current physical body at the appropriate time. This will become clear when this state of consciousness absorbs into your current state of mind. When this happens you awaken.

CAPTURE THE WIND

The concept of awakening may not make complete sense right now. Rest assured, any notion you may have of it does not compare to what it actually is.

Many misconceptions surround this state some of which will become clear in this book. The very nature of awakening makes it impossible to anticipate what it will be like. In fact, by creating expectations, you actually limit your ability to understand what lies ahead and make awakening more difficult.

What you are seeking is far beyond what you can currently imagine.

When you create expectations you are forming an idea about what the experience should be like, how long it should take for it to happen, and even how you will get there. What would have happened in the salmon story if you created an expectation about what the rivers and pools ahead of you should look like and then started coming across places that did not match that expectation? You would have believed you were going the wrong way and then turned around in discouragement.

Expectation can only be based on what you already know. In the end you are after what you cannot conceive. By looking for experiences you can relate to, you will overlook what you are truly searching for.

It is important to focus on the search, not the destination.

Pay attention to your actions, choose to be self-aware and try to stay conscious so that you will notice the deep moving feeling that comes from the Navigator.

As I said earlier you cannot follow the Navigator until you recognize it. By choosing to be self-aware and trying to listen to it, you acknowledge it. Acknowledging the Navigator is the first great step towards awakening. This means you realize that what you are reading makes sense to you because it does not make sense to everyone. It also means you accept there is a part of you that is separate from who you believe you are right now. This helps you to begin to step outside of yourself and the belief that you are the character in the book rather than the being reading it. The more you can acknowledge and accept this, the more you internalize it and it becomes a truth for you. Once that happens, while you may not consider it much now, it is a huge revelation spiritually. It will have an effect on you in the very near future and your whole perspective on reality will change. It allows the deeper part of your consciousness to begin to take control and helps lift you into the sky.

The goal initially, is to allow a clearer thought to emerge that will create a stronger connection to your higher consciousness. Every page of this book aids in strengthening that connection. Just as you stumbled upon many mysterious and amazing places in your journey following the strange instinct, so will the Navigator help you to have similar experiences. These moments are wonderful indeed and as you go through this book, you will even experience some of them.

There is purpose in your reading this book just as you have a higher purpose in this life so we must continue, as there is so much more to share. In this moment, you have to capture the wind; you do not have to ride it. You need to gather momentum and set your direction before you launch your journey of discovery. This book will give you the wind, the momentum, if you can set yourself to finish it. You may find that to be a more difficult task than it would seem. You may find many things suddenly arise that distract you and other obstacles, seemingly unrelated, pull you away from this knowledge.

You can overcome them. It is within your power to awaken. Make a commitment to yourself now to reach the end of this book. Make a commitment to capture the wind.

Capture the wind so that your Navigator can fulfill its purpose and steer you towards awakening.

When we awaken, we can better know our higher consciousness, which is a part of the larger 'Force'. It is difficult to find a term that comes close to adequately expressing what "IT" is really like without creating too many assumptions in people's minds.

When I say the Force, I mean the living energy that exists throughout the universe. It is a vibration, a frequency of energy, which connects us all together. We can also call this life force, this energy, God. Throughout this book, I will often refer to it as God. However, understand my meanings; I am trying to refer to different aspects of the same thing.

When I say God, I mean the part that is like a being, aware and conscious. You may imagine an old man with a long beard, ancient and wise beyond knowing but full of love and compassion. You may also imagine a woman, radiant with regal beauty; she is compassionate and full of knowledge. We can relate to this image as a human being.

The third way I will describe this "THING" is the Universe. When I say Universe, you may imagine planets, solar systems, and vast rotating galaxies. You may spin at the grandness of how large and vast a structure it truly is. It is the most physical aspect of the Force.

I will use all three of these terms at different times, the Force, God or the Universe but do not be confused because it is all the same thing.

You may ask why you feel a need to awaken. Those with the Navigator have a purpose and a specific destiny. What is *your* purpose? To understand your purpose you need to know how you fit into the larger scheme of things. You need to know how you are different from others. Notice I said different not better. Many people will assume, wrongly, that because I say that those of us with the Navigator are the minority and that we are different that I must mean we are better. It is not better or worse, it is simply different.

Do not deny this part of you.

Everything in life will make you question yourself. Except in your heart, deep down, you *know*. Your Navigator is trying to show you the way but you have to listen to it. You have to put everything you can on your side to awaken because the odds are stacked against you.

Where do you begin? You begin by trusting your Navigator. Allow it to reveal your purpose. Follow the path it sows you and embrace the unknown.

CHAPTER TWO

WAY OF THE WHITE CELL

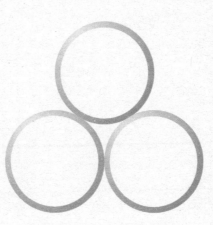

WAY OF THE WHITE CELL

You are aware of a sense within you that seemingly directs you as if it were a compass navigating your essence.

I wonder if you know yet why you are reading this book. I wonder if you question what led you to begin reading it in the first place. No doubt, you can think of many answers. All of them are probably very reasonable and logical. I am curious if you suspect yet, that there is another answer, which eludes you.

How long have you been searching, Navigator? How much longer will you question what lies within? I told you when we began that I had been searching for you for a very long time. Do you know why I would spend my life, all that I could give, trying to find you?

One reason, a very important one, is that we are so few and our purpose is precious and vital.

You can awaken. It is possible. The ways in which it will

transform not only your own life, but also the lives of those around you, is nothing short of miraculous. This transformation will help lead you to your destiny and it is important to me that you reach it. I can only help show you the way. You are the one who must walk it. The Navigator will also help lead you toward awakening but you must choose to follow it.

It is time to begin this journey.

THE WAY LESS TAKEN

The journey has many winding paths to explore. Many paths lead to dead-ends, others offer wonders to experience. The first step is to stop questioning your instincts. Recognize the Navigator and begin to follow where it leads. Your instincts will confirm what I have already told you.

You are different.

In the story of the salmon, a feeling inside moved you to question the world around you. It made you restless and set you out on your search. I told you about the beauty of the ocean, all there was to experience, and yet, for you, there was something missing. I told you there was something different about you for feeling this way because not everyone does.

To achieve awakening first realize what you are. Accept the reality of your destiny, become aware of it.

By becoming aware of the Navigator, it gives you the courage to be what you must. It will help you to find the strength to discover all that is within you. Awakening is a struggle because you must fight against the current. When you were a salmon you set out away from the ocean struggling against the rivers current. It required much more effort than drifting through the ocean. The thoughts, feelings, beliefs and views of the majority of people on this planet create a collective current. It is a collective consciousness.

Most of those who have the potential within them, who have a Navigator, will never reach awakening because of this current. Like salmon seeking out their place of origin, we know instinctively what to do, but we will be pushed along and lose our way. The collective consciousness of the planet will attempt to shape you. Awareness bestows strength. Awareness makes it possible to stand against the current and achieve your destiny.

People have different purposes in this world. Realize that people are different and no person is of greater value than another.

Every part of a greater whole is important. For example, the human body has many different organs all of which serve different functions. If you remove an organ, a heart, lung, stomach, or any other part, no matter how fancy or special the other parts may be there is going to be a big problem. Each functioning part has to be looked at as a contributing part of a greater whole. There are different individual parts for different purposes.

That is the problem we face now. Everyone is trying to do the same function and we are not contributing our separate roles. We do not realize people have different purposes.

We, you and I, must look at the purpose of people not from a human perspective but a universal one. All of our experiences in life will be unique. The contribution each of us makes to the world, the lives of those around us, and what we become in life is very different from our overall purpose and role in relation to the universe as a whole. When we broaden our perspective and look at it from the very large view of the entire universe the differences between the roles within humanity becomes very small.

To help us understand these differences we can use the cells of our own body as a rough analogy. First, let us divide the people of the world into two hypothetical groups, Red Cells and White Cells. Understand the distinction between these two terms. The world requires both types of people to maintain its existence. Our own bodies are the same. Both roles are important and essential for this planet's survival.

This planet will not exist without one or the other.

Think about what I just said. If at any time during our discussion, you doubt the importance of either role, return to what I just told you. If there is too much of one type and not enough of the other, or vice versa, much as your body would, the planet will slowly die. However, one group is much smaller than the other which makes the balance of their existence more delicate.

WHITE CELLS: FOR DEFENSE OF THE WHOLE

To understand Red Cells and White Cells look at the relationship that exists on all levels of this world. To understand something very large, look into something that is very small. Things of great magnitude and things of small stature reflect each other.

A parallel relationship exists in all things from macro to micro and micro to macro.

Begin to understand the Universe, which is very large, by looking inward, at ourselves, as we are very small. Think of the planet as a single thing. It may be made of many living things but try to imagine the interaction of all life on this planet as it might appear if seen from a great distance. From a distance, the planet looks like a single object. However, if we examine it closely all of the micro life overwhelms our concept of the Earth as a singular object. Nothing about the planet has changed. Our perspective has changed, which dramatically alters our concept of the planet.

You and I are the same. When you think of your body, you consider it one thing, but if we could zoom in, we would see a vast micro universe. Your body is really a collection of micro life and not a single object. The cells in your body are like living creatures. There are many different kinds with a huge variety of functions.

Your body is like the planet that we live on.

It is dependent on smaller systems of organisms to maintain it and help it to survive. The next time you are near a mirror, stop and take a good, long look. Put your face right up into the mirror and look as closely as you can at yourself. Do you know what makes up that 'thing' you are looking at in the mirror? Do you know what makes up 'you'?

The truth is, there is no single physical 'you' at all. Our physical selves are a vast grouping of living independent organisms that are working, more or less, for 'us' in a shared relationship.

Let us consider the connection between our mental self and our physical body. When we are depressed emotionally, our body's immune system can weaken in response. When we feel positive and happy, the strength of our immune system can increase. The consciousness of our being can have an effect on our physical body. Consciousness is a force that affects our body's inner universe. Our will can affect each cell, in some way.

However, not all cells are equally receptive to a person's will.

Some cells are more receptive than others. It is the same on the macro scale of the Earth. The Earth has a similar force that can affect all living things within it. This force is much like the immune system of our bodies. The planet is similar in some regards to us but also very alien. This is why I must use analogies to bridge the gap in comparing two very different things.

Two types of cells, red and white blood cells, are primarily found in our blood stream. Red Cells are vital for the mechanics of the body and make up the majority. They are responsible for servicing the body with oxygen and nutrients and repairing wounds. The role of the Red Cell is vital and necessary. But, they are completely unaware of the dangers of viruses and harmful bacteria.

White cells understand the dangers of viruses and spend their time seeking them out and opposing their destructive nature to the whole of the body. The abilities of a white cell are different from those of a red cell. Although they have some basic similarities, the functions that each type fulfills within the body are dramatically different. White cells can assess a virus before attacking it. They can also summon other white cells to assist with their assault. White cells even seem to possess a kind of memory of past battles with viruses. It is as if they are somehow able to pass on their knowledge and this helps them defend the body against similar viruses. Why is it you never catch the same cold twice? It is as if the knowledge, or essence, of the white cell passes on so that it may used to aid the whole in the future.

Those who possess the Navigator are the white cells of the planet.

Most of them are asleep and rarely awaken or even begin to realize their purpose. However, because they have a Navigator, they sense, deep in their heart, that there is some purpose, some role, which they must fulfill. Perhaps you are beginning to see why it is so important that they fulfill this purpose. In the micro world of the human body, viruses often overcome the body with disease or illness. This will happen in a similar way only on a larger scale if the White Cells of the Earth fail. Let this thought be a small reminder to aggressively seek your awakening.

Spiritual people of this planet serve as White Cells.

Those of us who possess a strong Navigator often feel an overwhelming sense of duty to serve the 'Force'. Intuitively we know that there will ultimately be a confrontation between ourselves and something else.

Spiritual people have a greater awareness of the planet's rhythm, they feel the life of the planet, and they are keen to it. These people are the protectors of the planet, and compose a higher level of sensory for it. Their desire to give and preserve life with a sense of compassion is very strong. These desires are essential qualities for the vital role of a White Cell. The Force instills these feelings to ensure the greatest chance that they will follow their nature and fulfill their purpose.

White Cells protect the planet, and the Red Cells within it, from the invasion of what you could call 'viruses'. Red Cells are, for the most part, oblivious to the 'outside' from which the invaders come.

White Cells, through their Navigator, have a sense of knowing that identifies a virus. Much in the same way that their Navigator directs them to awakening, their higher consciousness can also direct and warn them about viruses which might harm the whole. These viruses, if not dealt with, can infect the whole of the planet.

Planetary viruses can take many forms. They could be the cultural thought of a nation turned to war, widespread plagues, weapons designed to destroy great amounts of life and many other possibilities. They have similar traits, which make them anti-life, destructive or perhaps aid in the multiplication of a kind of life that eventually leads to death and decay, such as biological warfare.

White Cells fight these things so that life will continue and flourish.

They are different from doctors or aid workers who also seek to benefit life. White Cells work on multiple levels of reality. They may work in the physical world to protect life but more so, they seek to affect the spiritual. They do this with arcane knowledge that they acquire from White Cells that have come before. When an old White Cell dies, one who has a developed higher consciousness, they pass their experience on to the new White Cells. This helps the new generation to continue the battle and retain the knowledge of others. This process is much like reincarnation. Reincarnation is the concept in which the higher consciousness or an aspect of someone's being is reborn into a new body. Old White Cells reincarnate into new lives or to places where there is need of their knowledge from other battles.

Although this analogy may seem simplistic, black and white, there is profound truth to it.

Because of its simplicity, you should be able to understand the basics of it. Given the scale of what we are talking about this is an amazing thing! There are many layers to the things you and I discuss. These layers will become more evident to you in time, as the concepts are revealed further with thought and reflection.

Eventually you can expect to have sudden realizations, which will allow you to see things in ways that you never did before. You will be stunned by how you suddenly know more about things you thought you understood well. This happens when these concepts become a truth for you, as you begin to understand them on more than just an intellectual level. Everything I am talking about has layers, never assume you just 'get it' and move on. Give it thought, give it reflection and give it time.

Simple effort can bring astounding rewards.

The role of a White Cell is vital but it can also be very difficult. It is vital because without us the Earth and Red Cells are vulnerable. It is difficult because we are not born capable, aware and awakened.

A White Cell must struggle to awaken to fulfill its role.

Your choices and effort create a process that defines who you are. You have the Navigator to help guide you but this does not assure that you will ever take part in what you are meant to do!

The majority of the people on this planet are Red Cells and so it is easy for a White Cell to begin to live, act and think just like a Red Cell. You are not here for that! Because of the need to maintain the balance between the right amount of Red Cells and White Cells, it is part of the system of things that awakening is difficult. Only the most determined ever make it to any level of awakening.

There always exists the danger, however, that not enough White Cells will choose to serve their purpose by awakening, and the planet will be overcome with a 'virus' and die.

WHITE CELLS ARE NOT CHOSEN, THEY ARE MADE BY CHOICE

To really understand what a White Cell is and what it is capable of we will look at how it differs from a Red Cell. The Navigator is the part of the higher consciousness that directs a person into a process of awakening. You can think of this higher consciousness as an evolved consciousness of pure energy. It is created and refined over time through conscious, applied effort.

Members of the general human populace do not truly have a higher consciousness although everyone has the potential to develop one. This may be difficult to accept but please allow me to continue. You need to understand my definition of what a higher consciousness is before you can really consider what I am saying.

Humans have a sense of self, but, as science suggests, most people are no more than bio-chemical organic beings. Their level of communication and experiences occur only in the brain and are stored in an electrical consciousness.

This electrical consciousness is also made of energy but it is temporary. It is only capable of moving beyond the physical body after death with reflection and refinement. This separates an electrical body, which everyone has, from a higher consciousness, which a White Cell must develop.

The idea that everyone has an electrical body, but that this body is not the same as a higher consciousness or that White Cells may move on after death while Red Cells may not, may sound shocking. You may think I am suggesting that some people in your life, that you know and love, are without any connection to the Universe or that they will not receive the full experience of life.

Before you take such a position, consider what I am saying about the role of a White Cell.

White Cells are here to serve the Universe, a greater being, to ensure that the planet continues to grow, evolve and experience. They are here to serve and protect Red Cells and the planet as a whole. Red Cells also serve the Universe, a greater being, by contributing their lives and experiences to it by functioning for the planet.

The result is the same, only our roles differ.

You cannot measure the quality of life in human terms, whether you live one life or a million, the sum is still only a fraction of a second for the Universe. In the very far future, a ridiculous amount of time in terms of years, we will all return to the Force.

To truly understand what I am saying we need to discuss what a higher consciousness is. Although I certainly respect emotions, feelings, intentions, love and passion, I feel that these are very complex abilities of the human brain. These characteristics do not require a higher consciousness to exist within a person.

A higher consciousness is born through a series of revelations.

We begin by contemplating our existence, the meaning of the self, and eventually have the revelation that the body is not who we truly are or at least not all that we could be. The next revelation is that perhaps another body exists. This other body is the higher consciousness and just the act of imagining this other body creates the higher consciousness's existence within you.

The act of imagining a higher consciousness and reflecting on the nature of a person's existence is like exercise for a person's higher consciousness. By reflecting on the inner-dimensions of your body's energy and higher consciousness, you make your higher consciousness stronger.

This reflection increases the energy available for use throughout the body.

Energy used for touch, smell, or taste takes on a life of its own and collectively becomes alive. It becomes a living conscious being; separate, but still a part of you.

The higher consciousness is a body with many dimensional opportunities but this is the easy part. Once you establish the body of the higher consciousness the next, more difficult, step is to ensure that you satisfy its needs. Just as the physical body requires nutrition and exercise to grow, so the higher consciousness also requires things to grow and mature.

To become a true White Cell we must exercise our other body, we must exercise our higher consciousness.

A White Cell must seek out awakening by obtaining knowledge and practicing techniques. You must be dedicated to a path if you expect to awaken. There are seven different kinds of bodies, the first of which is flesh. This immediate physical body is composed of a person's bone, blood and all of the matter and organisms that constitute what you would typically think of as your self.

The second body is the electrical field within your body. This electrical body makes your eyes blink and your mouth move. It keeps your heart ticking and your lungs expanding and contracting.

Foods that you eat which contain energy, originally gathered through photosynthesis from captured sunlight, create your electrical body. Your current electrical body is the recreation of this basic solar energy.

The higher consciousness that we have been talking about is really the third body. As I stated before, most people only have the first two bodies, one that is flesh and one that is more like electricity. With standard religious beliefs, most people do not put forth the effort that is required to create the third body.

These beliefs teach that everyone is suddenly born with a vessel or consciousness that continues after death. It is out of ignorance that they believe they can obtain one without any effort. It is as if they are automatically given one by some kind of Acme energy consciousness, or soul-press, right out of some old cartoon. Ka-boom, here's your soul, ka-boom, here's your soul.... everybody gets one! It's a giant higher consciousness factory! No work and no effort involved!

This is simply not how the Universe works.

An individual must create a higher consciousness. It is not something that everyone is born with. There is no way to manifest a higher consciousness without first applying effort to the process that is required to create it. This concept directly contradicts what most religions teach.

I cannot hide the truth for fear of controversy. It is what it is.
When a person without a higher consciousness dies, their energy returns to the Force. They return to God by merging into the planet's collective consciousness, like a sugar cube thrown into the ocean. For Red Cells, this is necessary and needed, but it is a bad

thing for a White Cell because it means you have not fulfilled your purpose.

When this happens to a White Cell it means they have failed to awaken and failed to commit enough effort to reincarnate. A White Cell must choose to achieve a higher consciousness, or not. Any person is ultimately free to choose to reject what I am saying and to walk away and believe whatever they like. But, as a White Cell, this choice assures that you will never fulfill your purpose.

The creation of the third body requires effort in the form of active self-reflection.

It requires devotion to exercise the other bodies, to exercise your higher consciousness. The Universe gave us Navigators to ensure that we would have a sense, a need, to seek it out and find it. It also gives us a choice, it gives everyone a choice, either we want to seek it out or we do not.

Be assured, we have free will to choose our path.

PLANTING THE SEED OF ETERNITY

Our third body, much like our brain, has a form of intelligence. Its creation comes through work and effort and as you apply yourself and put forth energy, it becomes stronger. It grows stronger by thinking about your body and realizing how mechanical your body is. This leaves another presence and that presence makes you more aware of yourself.

This awareness grows as your higher consciousness develops through time and effort. This is no different from other living things. A seed planted in the soil needs nurturing to grow. It needs food, water and attention. If given these things, it will slowly push up from the ground, spread its leaves and blossom. Should your eternal energy being, your higher consciousness, be any different?

Anything living that grows has stages of development. The higher consciousness is no different.

This process of development is reflected, to varying degrees, in White Cells and Red Cells. Do not think you can simply lump people into two large categories. I do so for the sake of simplicity but it is not how the world truly is. There are degrees.

Red Cells, who surround themselves with very spiritual people, can create a higher consciousness, allowing them to reincarnate. You also have very new White Cells and very old ones. I consider many spiritual people I have met in my journeys to be White Cells.

They are truly devoted to assisting the world and mankind.

The Navigator of a White Cell will tell them what they truly are. This knowledge leaps out in their heart as truth. Usually they are young and lack the ability to take control of the direction of their life. Pressure from friends and family to adopt certain beliefs makes it even more difficult but those that have the will must make attempts at this direction.

At any stage in your life, when you feel the pull of the Navigator, it is only through an act of will that you set yourself in motion.

Many people become fickle, thinking that if something goes wrong or does not seem right that it must be a 'sign' from the Universe that this is not right. Well, if every bump in the road makes you change course then no, it is not for you, because life will try to hinder your awakening. When a salmon tries to swim upstream and return home they do so struggling against the current with many obstacles in their way.

You too must go against the current to fulfill your purpose.

The current that keeps you from moving forward is what I call the machine, meaning you are afraid of the unexpected and unknown and society's programming holds you in place.

It is said that when the student is ready the teacher appears. A teacher can take many different forms. This book, in a sense, is a teacher. It is here to assist, guide, and encourage you toward awakening. That is my intention with what you are reading now. I want to guide, assist and encourage you. In the end, it is up to you to decide what to do with this knowledge.

It is foolish to question whether you are one of us, you already know.

You also already know what you must do. Let us continue on our way by pushing further into the macro and understand in detail how the planet and its collective consciousness affect us all. Awareness is your key to open the door of higher consciousness. Use this knowledge to empower it. Remember, it is in the most unlikely of times that you will find what you are really looking for. Now that you are more "awake" try to stay there lest you fall back asleep and forget this all.

CHAPTER THREE

THE WORLD IS ALIVE

THE WORLD IS ALIVE

This navigator gives you a sense of knowing; directing you away from the trappings of mans religions and structured thinking.

The world is alive. Our planet, a shining solitary globe floating in inky black space is a living organism. Do not be fooled by the simplicity of this. Earth, this organism that we are a part of, is a being that is completely alien to us. Try not to allow yourself to simply gaze over each sentence. I did not just say the planet is alive, meaning that it bears life and life forms populate it. That is obviously true. I mean that the Earth is a living organism, a being, floating in space. It is an amazing realization, to fully understand the nature of this being and what our connection to it is!

Everything is connected. To understand who you are you must examine every level of the universe from the very small to the very large. They are all reflections of each other. You are more than your body. You are a single living organism made of billions of individual organisms. Earth is more than the physical structure that makes up the planet.

THE REFLECTION CONNECTION

To better illustrate this idea, imagine you are on a tropical island somewhere in the Pacific Ocean completely isolated from any other land. This is not a small island it is huge! It is gigantic! Lush jungle, with towering green trees wrapped in twisting, flowering vines that cover the island. All kinds of foliage fills this jungle, it teems with life. Butterflies float and flutter through the air as colorful birds swoop among the trees.

Bending down you see red and black ants crawling on the ground and through the foliage. Glancing up towards the treetops, you notice delicate spider webs hanging in the trees sparkling in the sun. Whenever you examine something closely, there is another form of life existing there, completely unaware of you or the massive island you are on.

Curious to see more of the island you find a tree that towers above all of the others and begin to climb it. You climb until you are high in the air above the canopy of trees. Far below you see a white sandy beach that falls down to the ocean. In the other direction, you can see tall mountain peaks jutting out of the sprawling jungle. You think to yourself, my god, it would take forever to explore this island. It could take weeks and weeks just to take it all in. It is so huge. You can see everything from distant mountain peaks barely visible on the horizon to all the micro life moving through the jungle below. You can see everything on a larger and smaller scale. Suddenly you are aware of the micro-verse moving into the macro-verse. You notice a boat floating in the water down on the shore and decide to take a boat ride.

You go down to the shore, wade into the clear water, and launch the boat. You crank up the motor and the boat zooms out to sea as you sit back and drink a Piña Colada and look at the island. Smiling you can feel the warm sunlight shining down and take it all in.

Moving further and further out to sea the island blurs and the details of its features merge. The boat begins moving faster. Speeding along you look back and the island becomes smaller and smaller against an expanding horizon. Now it looks like one large object in the distance, a big stone structure.

It looks like one, single thing.

If you suddenly zoomed back into the forest on the island, life in hundreds of forms would surround you, and you could take in all of the details. Zooming back out again, all of the small details merge into a single large structure.

The island is one single object, from a certain perspective, but millions of separate things make it up. The Earth is also one single object, from a certain perspective in outer space, but billions of separate individual things make it up.

All things in the universe reflect this model.

Now try to examine the same concept in another way. Think about if you were to take a syringe and insert the needle into your arm to draw out blood. First, you insert the needle then you pull the syringe and fill the chamber with a tiny amount of blood. If a blood cell was intelligent enough to realize what was happening it could float up to the glass of the syringe and say, 'Where are all the other blood cells?! Where's Harry the white cell?! Where's Julie the red cell?! Where is everybody?!' Then it would take one look at you and wonder, 'What the hell is this one big giant thing with flapping tentacles coming from its body?' Pushing the syringe the blood cell shoots back into the bloodstream, it goes back into your inner-verse, and it sees all of its friends again.

Observing your body, even if these cells were intelligent they would have no way to relate to what you are. The concept that you are a conscious, active, aware being with a body and that they are a part of your body is not conceivable to them. How could they possibly relate, their whole world is about other blood cells? Their world consists of moving oxygen and nutrients around your blood stream. Your body and everything about you would appear completely alien to them.

When I say the Earth is a living being I mean that it is also conscious. It is aware. It is a being far different than we are and its thoughts so alien to our own way of thinking it is difficult to even consider them thoughts. Yet, it is so.

MOVING BEYOND THE HUMAN PERSPECTIVE

The planet, Earth, and the universe do not have arms or legs, but we should consider them living things. Why does the planet or the universe need to have arms and legs to be a singular living being? Why does something have to be micro to be living, when it could be absolutely larger than we are? Why do we only recognize as living beings those things that are smaller than, or about the same size as, we are? Beings can be microscopic, or absolutely larger than us. Only our concept of what a conscious being is limits our understanding.

The planet and the universe are living organisms. They are living beings.

When you take a break from reading this book go walk outside and think about our micro perspective. Walk around and be aware of every level that life operates on. Reflect on how limited human perspectives are. Think about the cells moving inside your body. See the lanes of cars moving down the freeways, carrying cargo to build new structures. Think about seeing those cars from the air, up in a helicopter or an airplane. Tiny little blobs moving down long narrow structured streets like veins. See the people inside those vehicles they transmit ideas and information. They carry fuel, and food, which are the nutrients of society. The truth of this is all around you! Let this truth become you. It will set you free.

Now we come to the good news and bad news. Presumably, you

want to hear the bad news first. The bad news is; the dilemma our imaginary blood cell faced, when trying to comprehend what we are, is similar to the dilemma that we face, when trying to understand how the Earth or the universe can be alive. The struggle is not to simply acknowledge that there is life within them, which makes them living things, that is easy to accept. The struggle is in trying to comprehend that they are *conscious* living things and *how* such a conscious being would think and experience. It is difficult for us to comprehend how things of such magnitude can be conscious.

For the sake of simplicity let us narrow our scope to just the Earth. The Earth is a system so vast and beyond our conception that we simply cannot comprehend it in the same way that we normally comprehend things. Our minds struggle to envision a being that so exceeds our human scale.

The good news is that because the laws of nature repeat themselves at all levels we can use our micro to macro examples to help us at least begin to grasp the aspects that are most relevant to our own lives. In truth, it is possible to tap into the consciousness of the Earth. To understand what this means, we now have to consider what consciousness is.

As you read this text, you are conscious. You are having a mental experience while reading these words and you are aware. What are you aware of? You are certainly aware of the words printed on this page. Perhaps you are aware of secondary thoughts going through your mind. Maybe you feel happy or perhaps you are hungry, and if so, you would be aware of that as well.

Are you aware of the sound of birds or traffic or other sounds? If so, then you are aware of the environment around you. I hope that all the other things you are aware of are in the background now because you should be focused on reading this!

Now consider who or what it is that is aware. Where, exactly, is the 'you' that is aware? Can you point to the exact place? Is it in, on, or outside of your body that contains this awareness that you feel? It can be tricky to talk about consciousness. To this day, it continues to boggle the minds of most philosophers and scientists.

Consciousness is more than just the body, the design and purpose of which is to provide us with experience. Imagine driving a car. Our eyes see the inside of the car, the road ahead of us, other cars around us, the sky, clouds, and anything else that enters our field of vision. Our ears hear the engine of our car, the music playing through the stereo, and words from the person in the passenger seat. Our hands feel the warmth of the sun and the wind as it blows through the car. Our whole body feels the affect of inertia on us when we make a turn. The amount of data our body processes is really quite phenomenal. As all of this data is coming in through our sensory organs, our body is doing some amazing things with it. In the end, however, the body converts all of this information into electrical energy.

The reason our body converts sensory data into electricity is that, by nature we are an energy being.

The body makes experiences possible and there are many levels to them. For example, while we are driving a car we are holding the steering wheel. At the lowest level, the nerves that run through our fingers are individually registering the fact that there is something going on. Through a complex process of electro-chemical interactions, they transmit what they are each experiencing. The individual experiences of millions of these cells combine to form a series of nerve impulses that travel from our fingers to our arm, to our spine, and ultimately to our brain. Even one of these impulses, which contains only the smallest fragment of what will become our experience of holding the steering wheel, is in turn experienced by all of our nerves along the route from our fingers to our brain. Our brain receives and processes these impulses. Cells in our brain receive arriving impulses and decide how to best deal with incoming information. After the brain collects sufficient information, we might actually experience a conscious thought like, "Hey, the steering wheel is hot!"

To be perfectly clear, a multitude of individual cells in our bodies receive even the subtlest of experiences.

It is because of the experiences of individual micro-life in our bodies that we are able to have experiences. This means your consciousness, who you believe you are right now, is really the result of all the collected experiences of the micro-life that makes up your body.

They are sharing their experiences with you and that has formed your consciousness.

You are, in a sense, the collective consciousness of millions of micro-organisms and cells. Here the question must be asked: Why does it have to stop there? Is it possible that individual human experiences roll up to higher and higher levels to provide experiences for something greater than ourselves? It is possible and it is so.

ONE CONSCIOUSNESS, MANY EXPERIENCES

Astronauts floating in space agree that when looking down at the planet they can no longer relate to their houses, swimming pools, or to their friends and family. The Earth looks like one living thing, one living being, and the ancient word for it is Gaia. Gaia is the name for the being of the Earth. Gaia is a conscious living being and mankind is the nervous system of that being. Lives are the experiences of Gaia. Thoughts and emotions are accumulated and form a collective being; a collective consciousness.

The total collective thoughts of every conscious thing on this planet form the consciousness of the planet. This is the collective consciousness.

Multitudes of frequencies, each unique to a species, create this consciousness. The collective consciousness of human beings is on a different wavelength than say, dogs or monkeys or other organisms. They are like different radio stations. One species is 106.7 while another is 98.5. Every frequency is exclusive to a specific species. Every individual within a species also has a specific, unique frequency. No two beings on this planet share an identical frequency.

Using the above example, if the collective consciousness of all the monkeys on the planet was 106.7 then we could also say each monkey would have a slight variation of that frequency. One monkey might be 106.72 and another 106.78. While I do not intend for the example frequencies to be precise, it is important to note that every single consciousness vibrates at a unique frequency, never to be duplicated.

There are scientists who are moving forward and making progress in understanding and proving this concept. They might not be there yet, but their research, and the work of others like them, will someday lead to the discovery of a collective consciousness. In the future, it will just be a commonly known fact. 'Oh, of course the planet has a collective consciousness', any elementary school student will be able to tell you.

Biologist Rupert Sheldrake writes about the existence and explanation of a collective consciousness in many of his works. He asserts that collective consciousness only makes sense if there is also such a thing as collective memory: the storage of information as the species grows and evolves.

Sheldrake, who is primarily a biologist, talks about something that most people may have never considered as anything other than elementary. That is; how does a seed grow into a full grown plant? How do embryos develop from fertilized eggs? At first these sound like very basic, very simple questions. With our vast and magnificent understanding of the universe, surely this is something we can easily explain. But biologists disagree about how we can explain this seemingly simple phenomenon.

Imagine a little acorn planted in the ground. The form and shape of that little acorn, hidden in the earth, is vastly different from the giant tree it will become, with branches sticking out in every direction, leaves and bark, roots reaching far into the earth. We could say that the acorn contains some kind of genetic program that tells it how to grow and how to form. But, where is this program? If we said this genetic program was within the DNA science, and biologists such as Rupert Sheldrake, tell us we would be wrong. DNA codes for proteins and the micro components which make up proteins.

Coding the structure of single, solitary parts that make up organisms, such as proteins, is very different than coding the shape and structure of an entire organism.

Sheldrake gives an excellent example when he considers the make-up of the human body. Look at one of your arms. Twist your arm, move your fingers around and examine everything your arm can do. Now look at one of your legs. Bend your leg, move it around and examine everything your leg can do. Both look different, do different things and are in different places on your body. Yet the building blocks which create your arms and legs are the same. On a cellular level, there is no difference, so how did they become different? Why do they appear different and serve different functions? How did that come to be?

Sheldrake proposes a theory he calls Morphic Resonance. This theory basically states that there is a field of energy surrounding and permeating an organism which contains, among other things, the form of the organism. He writes that each species has its own field, that there are fields within fields, and that these fields have built-in memory, based upon what has happened in the past derived from previous organisms or forms of a similar kind. In other words, each organism on the planet shares fields of similar energy or we could say, a specific frequency just like we discussed earlier. We can see where science is starting to catch up. In his book, A New Science of Life, Sheldrake describes one such incident that he suggests proves this idea of Morphic Resonance, or as I prefer, collective consciousness.

"The best documented of these is the behavior of bluetits, a rather small bird with a blue head, that is common throughout Britain. Fresh milk is still delivered to the door each morning in Britain. Until about the 1950s, the caps on the milk bottles were made of cardboard. In 1921 in Southampton, a strange phenomenon was observed. When people came out in the morning to get their milk bottles, they found little shreds of cardboard all around the bottom of the bottle, and the cream from the top of the bottle had disappeared. Close observation revealed that this was being done by bluetits, who sat on top of the bottle, pulled off the cardboard with their beaks, and then drank the cream. Several tragic cases were found in which bluetits were discovered drowned head first in the milk!

This incident caused considerable interest; then the event turned up somewhere else in Britain, about 50 miles away, and then somewhere about 100 miles away. Whenever the bluetit phenomenon turned up, it started spreading locally, presumably by imitation. However, bluetits are very home-loving creatures, and they don't normally travel more than four or five miles. Therefore, the dissemination of the behavior over large distances could only be accounted for in terms of an independent discovery of the habit. The bluetit habit was mapped throughout Britain until 1947, by which time it had become more or less universal. The people who did the study came to the conclusion that it must have been "invented" independently at least 50 times. Moreover, the rate of spread of the habit accelerated as time went on. In other parts of Europe where milk bottles are delivered to doorsteps, such as Scandinavia and Holland, the habit also cropped up during the 1930s and spread in a similar manner. Here is an example of a pattern of behavior which was spread in a way which seemed to speed up with time, and which might provide an example of morphic resonance.

But there is still stronger evidence for morphic resonance. Because of the German occupation of Holland, milk delivery ceased during 1939-40. Milk deliveries did not resume until 1948. Since bluetits usually live only two to three years, there probably were no bluetits alive in 1948 who had been alive when milk was last delivered. Yet when milk deliveries resumed in 1948, the opening of milk bottles by bluetits sprang up rapidly in quite separate places in Holland and spread extremely rapidly until, within a year or two, it was once again universal. The behavior spread much more rapidly and cropped up independently much more frequently the second time round than the first time. This example demonstrates the evolutionary spread of a new habit which is probably not genetic but rather depends on a kind of collective memory due to morphic resonance."

I could continue with many other examples, but by now, you should begin to understand the importance of this idea. This concept is not something you should just let idly pass by as only an, 'interesting idea.' Think about it.

Consider that you are not simply an individual, but part of a greater system, a collective being.

The collective consciousness affects each of us and those who come after us whether we want it to or not. Your actions and thoughts connect to the whole just as the whole connects to you. What are you contributing to this collective? How will your life affect the thoughts of all of us? Do not believe you are insignificant.

Each of your actions and thoughts pass to the collective consciousness.

Each species on this planet has a collective consciousness within its own species, whales, dolphins, lions, beavers, and even human beings in a very complex way. The energy consciousness of each species is constantly moving around the globe and makes up the consciousness, collectively, of the planet.

It is the consciousness of Gaia.

The same way we have billions of living microscopic creatures telling us what is going on so does every living thing do the same for Gaia. We have cells and nerves, and even a nerve is made out of millions of living molecules. Cells can contract and expand and react to different impulses allowing electrons to have a form of data created by their consciousnesses collectively building as other nerves add to that information until it gets to one central processing point, you. We serve the same function for the planet.

THAT WHICH CONNECTS, TIES AND BINDS US ALL TOGETHER

We have an energy field that radiates from our body. We also know that plants have it and we know that all objects radiate energy as well. What we have also found, which is amazing, is that there is an energy field that covers the planet even over the deserts and the deepest parts of the ocean. This energy field is a soul or a sense of being, whatever you want to call it.

One being, one consciousness, and one soul but made of many individual living things.

The Universe is no different, only the size and perspective changes. Now imagine you are back on the giant island, except this time you are boarding a spaceship. Blasting away from Earth into dark space, you can see the whole planet floating beneath you. You can no longer look around in any direction and see land, hills, or mountains because there is only space. Consider how it would feel and look to have the whole planet floating below you as one living thing. Moving around inside this one thing are all the micro-verses, the red and white cells of human beings and cats and dogs and whatever else might be there, billions of living organisms, like you and I. Just like your body.

Now the spaceship turns to point out towards space and for the sake of this analogy, imagine that the spaceship can move faster than the speed of light.

Now as before on the boat, you are sitting on the back of the spaceship sipping your piña colada as the spaceship rockets through the universe. You look at the planet, and you cannot help but admire it as the spaceship moves into space. You go past all of the planets, solar systems, and quickly shoot out of our galaxy and head into the universe and the cosmos. It does not stop there, so you keep going and going.

As you keep going from this tiny, little molecular section of the whole universe you move through all of it until you get to what I would consider, 'the edge'. This is the edge of the entire universe.

You push the spaceships' turbo thrusters and shoot out beyond the edge of the universe into pure infinity, pure nothing. You look around and there are no planets, no stars, no nothing, it is a void of nothingness. You sit in the back of the spaceship and look through the window back at the universe, you see sparkles everywhere, billions of sparkles; those are stars, the suns. As you move further away, like the island and the Earth, you see the edges of the expanding universe. As you move even further away, it gets smaller and more condensed and starts to look like a big, glowing, globular, single, object floating in pure black.

That is God. That is the body of God.

Everything inside of it is matter, as we are matter. God's soul, prana, the Force, is the energy that intertwines it all. It is what interconnects it, and permeates all things.

The universe began with something like the Big Bang. There was a giant explosion of gases and other things that created mass and condensed molecules. This explosion is forever expanding. Billions and billions of years ago this happened and now its movement has slowed. Although it is slower, it is still expanding.

What is it expanding into? It is expanding into absolute nothingness, a pure infinite black with no planets, no stars, and no meteorites, not even dust. This expanding glob has borders and matter inside of it, much like our body.

Similarly, our body exists in and moves around in a kind of nothingness. Everything that we consider ourselves to be is contained within the boundary of our expanding body, which has been growing since infancy and began smaller than a microbe within a womb. We have expanded. Just as we expand, so the universe is expanding. All things in the universe are reflections of each other from the very small to the unimaginably enormous.

Man exists in the image of God but in a much different way than we ever could expect.

Not with hands and feet, but as an inner-cosmos made out of different organ systems, yet co-operating and working together to create a synchronicity among separate parts which together form one being. From micro-verse to macro-verse, it repeats.

Now that I have gone so far to explain the body of God, no doubt your curiosity is pushing you to think about another question. It is a question that is always asked of me, and your Navigator too, wants to know. If the Big Bang created the physical matter in the universe, which is the body of God how did the Big Bang come to be? How did the Force come to be here? Where is the source of that energy which your Navigator feels and knows as home? I think it is time to finally answer this question. Let us push on.

THE CREATION OF GOD

THE CREATION OF GOD

It is elusive to structural thinking.

Where did everything come from? This ultimate question has bewildered philosophies and religions. How many times have you contemplated the origin of our existence or wondered what the first moments of creation were like? We are about to embark on a journey for the answer to this ultimate question.

The very nature of what we are about to discuss is so abstract that it is a very difficult question to attempt to answer in simple language. Most philosophies do not even try to answer this question. They simply state that there are limits to the things that man can know. Many religious traditions suggest that we should not even try to find an answer! They choose to believe it is beyond our capacity to know the nature and workings of God. If a question is difficult to answer, does this mean we should not ask it? If a question has yet to be answered does this mean that we should accept that there is no answer?

We should not accept this kind of thought. Yet often we do.

Many who came before us said there were no real answers to the ultimate question because they did not know them. While scientists build devices that allow them to see far beyond what the naked eye allows, we create internal walls that prevent our minds from doing the same.

We do not question what lies within, and we do not encourage our consciousness to develop and evolve. Others have constructed walls that confine our consciousness and separate us from the universe and we have accepted them. Yet, I know that the universe gave me a brain with an intellect and free will so that I could ask questions and discover answers.

BREAKING DOWN THE WALLS WITHIN

Do you want to know how God works and thinks? How would that alter the way you view everything in life? Maybe you doubt such a thing as God, even exists. Perhaps in doubting you are questioning, and in the end, you still hope to find an answer. You just cannot yet conceive of or understand what that answer might be.

If I could know how God works and thinks, it would be an amazing feat don't you think? How can I dare to suggest that, without the use of highly technical equipment, I can explain the creation of God?

Well, to begin with, I did not accept that I could not know such a thing.

To answer the ultimate question we first need to break everything down in a way that it is possible to understand. The difficulty is this: the moment I try to reduce the, 'nature of everything' into a simple concise form it loses much of its meaning. Words cannot accurately express some things. Due to the structural way our brains work it is difficult to comprehend those things not limited by the physical or structural laws of matter; things that are dimensional or energetic in nature.

Infinity is one such concept.

Time without limit, or existence without time, is a notion that is almost inconceivable to our way of thinking. We understand what the word means and we can get an idea of the concept but beyond that we cannot grasp it. The difficulty is that time is so ingrained in measuring every aspect of our lives that most people cannot conceive existing outside of it. This is why the answer to the question that seems unanswerable may leave you with mixed feelings.

Part of you may be amazed at what I am about to present, but at the same time, you may lack total satisfaction because you sense another part eludes you. The answer may seem somehow incomplete. You do not have to accept this feeling of missing the total picture. However, you do need to accept that there are limitations to what the human brain can conceive.

Understanding has levels.

To be aware of and really get what I am about to tell you, on different levels, will take time and reflection. Some knowledge also requires more of an energy or dimensional consciousness to understand and experience what it is. The creation of God is that kind of knowledge. To understand it, I mean really know it, to the point that you experience it, requires consciousness. I know that by reading this, and beginning to grasp it, you will have enough of the picture that it will change you.

There is no turning back now. By reading on you will be fully committed. Are you ready?

BEFORE THE BIG BANG

In the beginning, there was absolute nothingness, pure black, pure infinite space. There was no dust or planets, no stars or gaseous forms, no light at all, not even particles or atoms. There was nothing. Absolute, infinite nothingness stretched forever. The void was complete. No matter existed at all. Because there was nothing, there was one other 'thing' and that was an opposing force, there has to be. That other thing was a vacuum, which is the vacuum of space.

Imagine the vacuum of space to be, quite literally, a kind of pressure. It has an intense and powerful pull. For example, if you take the hose from a vacuum cleaner and then press it against the palm of your hand you can feel its suction pulling on you. There is a draw or some kind of a pull, and that pull is a pressure.

Of course, in this example a machine is generating suction, which is quite different from what we are talking about. However, the feeling of how it pulls on you should give you an idea to work with.

In the beginning, because there was nothing, it would be like sucking all the air out of a Ziploc bag. It crumples and begins to fold in on itself. Of course, this image is very limited because you picture a small plastic Ziploc bag that has edges, which does not completely work for what we are trying to visualize so you have to take that example and move way beyond that.

It may be easier to picture blowing a Ziploc bag full of air first, which would be like an expanding universe with energy moving into it. Now contrast that image by, once again, picturing all of the air being pulled out. The bag would flatten and begin to crumple, collapse inward, and finally implode. You see, because the void is so big and so heavy it creates a vacuum out of itself, it is pulling on itself. That is the hardest part to explain to someone. If you can get past that and envision an infinite space with enormous pressure, you have an idea of the beginning.

Let us take another quick example. If you were to teleport, which means to instantaneously disappear and then reappear, in the middle of space at the beginning of time, or the beginning of anything, the second you appeared you would have been torn into a billion pieces infinitely smaller than molecules.

It would have sucked you apart.

It would have exploded you beyond even nano-particles. Do you understand? It is because the pressure was so intense. You need to imagine that kind of force and power.

It is incredible to conceive.

The nothing and the vacuum acted against each other and created enormous tension. These two elements resembled opposing forces pressing against one another, but no matter existed, so the only evidence of this tension was the creation of an energy. This tension-force was an energy, of sorts, and was the only property of infinity. It was not a thing. It was not matter and had no kind of physical form.

It permeated the infinite void.

As you visualize this tension, you could say it was a kind of friction but more intense and even beyond friction, imagine the friction between these two infinite forces creating an equally infinite source of energy by the very act of tension between them! It was all of this 'pulling' that created a kind of energy, which we will just call free electrons only because it needs a name.

This tension, this intense friction, created billions of free electrons forever and ever and ever! Try to imagine oceans of entire universes making this path, like red smoke, thicker than water, and you will get an idea of it. Of course, because you or I cannot see it with our eyes, because it is so fine, absolutely beyond even microscopic, beyond molecular, it is almost impossible for us to conceive how much of it there was! It was so intensely FULL because that was all that existed!

For infinity, all that existed was this energy created by the pull of the universe.

We have been talking about the beginning of things, but this is misleading because without matter time cannot exist. The universe, as we are imagining it now, existed before matter so there would be no time. The beginning is before God existed in this dimension, before anything existed. Although it may sound strange, what eventually happened in this infinite nothing was simply 'something'.

Something happened because something must always happen. It is a numbers game.

Consider another numbers game, the lottery. If you played the lottery, do you think you would win this week? You would probably say no. What if you played once a week for the rest of your life, do you think you could win before you died? Again, you would answer probably not. These questions are easy to answer because the odds of winning the lottery are so overwhelmingly against any particular individual.

Now imagine that you are an immortal who will live forever, and you have a desire to play the lottery every day of your never-ending existence. You have nothing else to do with eternity, right? Now can you expect to win? Absolutely, you would have to. Eventually you would win because even if the odds were one in eighteen million you could play for eighteen million days. One of those days during your eternal life, you would hit the jackpot.

The infinite void is much the same.

In the infinite void before the universe, eventually, something is going to happen. The key to understanding that 'something' must happen is to understand that the absence of time makes 'something' happening not a probability, but an undeniable certainty. This is providing all the proper circumstances are in place and in this particular case, they were.

THE SPARK OF CREATION

To understand the 'something' that happened; imagine that we have a super-powerful microscope. With this instrument, we can closely examine what things looked like before anything happened. If we were to zoom in and examine all of those free electrons I spoke of earlier we could see what would look like little flat square flakes that dimly glow red.

If you have ever eaten ice cream, usually mint, with little chocolate chip flakes that is what these flakes resemble. Remember, they were not actually made of anything yet. They were like particles of energy, not matter. They were everywhere, billions and billions of them forever. They would vibrate gently back and forth in a uniform direction and move so slowly, that even if we could see them, we could not measure their movement.

Eventually what happened in this moment of 'something' is a single shimmering red flake collided with another and created something like the shape of the letter 'T'. They connect with one being the top of the 'T' and the other forming the center.

After colliding with each other these two, now entwined, flakes stopped shimmering and began to rotate in the opposite direction from all the other flakes. This generated a different kind of electrical current and, once activated, it began to grow. It begins with just the two flakes but as it slowly vibrated against everything else, it grew, the way a tiny snowball will grow when rolling down a steep hill. It gathered and accumulated other flakes and began to create an electrical pulse. This reaction creates a different kind of electron, a different kind of pulse of energy that resembles electricity.

This electricity, unhindered by any other force acting on it, became a living thing. As electricity, as energy, nothing could affect it, not the tension or friction, nothing. The void was still there which meant the pull of the universe was still creating tension, which created the red flake energy. This new growing electrical pulse consumed, in a sense, the red flake energy, which stretched throughout the void forever. It had no mind, no consciousness, or any purpose at that point but it was suddenly growing and alive.

Like something in a womb, it was infinitely small, but contained a spark of creation, a spark that eventually became you and became all other forms of matter as it grew to become absolutely enormous in comparison to its beginning.

Let us use our Ziploc bag again to help us imagine this in a structured way. While not entirely accurate, it helps our brain be able to grab hold of the concept and work with it. Imagine taking an empty Ziploc bag and rubbing the two sides together. Do you know what happens when you do this? You create static electricity. One side of the bag represents the nothingness of the void. The other side is the vacuum.

When we rub the two sides together, there is friction, which is a kind of energy and represents our red flakes. Now at some moment, this friction begins to create static electricity, a kind of energy. Like our new energy even the static of the Ziploc is totally separate from the bag, does not fill it, does not influence it, yet is all around it and generated by the friction created by those two initial elements.

While this energy was infinitely smaller than matter, its growth was still measurable, which means a form of time existed. Although this form of time was so different from how we understand it now, for the sake of creating a timeline we can understand, we will make use of the word.

Over vast amounts of time, this mass became more complex and used as fuel these red shimmering flakes of energy. It continued to attach, multiply, and expand itself, becoming increasingly complicated as its energy rose in vibration, until it became a form of living energy. It grew more complex, drawing together atom-like structures, and creating different energy forms. These structures spiraled around other electron-like structures, their movements becoming more complex, until they created the very first foundation, or building blocks, of what would become matter.

At first, these were very faint levels of matter-like material. They were more energy than physical material, and they had very complex forms but were still contained in this enormous thing, this cloud or gaseous organism of energy.

From the nothing, something was born, it grew, and eventually it became intelligent.

DECIPHERING THE LANGUAGE OF THE UNIVERSE

This intelligence, however, was so different and still is so different, so alien, to our form of intelligence that it is hard to conceive. I will try to explain it in a way that expresses the overall idea of it.

Numbers can explain the universe. They are the galactic code of the whole universe.

Numbers are a completely separate language. This galactic code is composed of mathematical patterns that all things follow in the universe. Now putting that aside for a moment we can understand the patterns of things in terms of their rhythm, which can be translated into numbers.

In other words, everything that has a rhythm has a number. The rhythm creates a pattern, which also has a number. The pattern is like a beat. Just as we can count out a beat, we can assign numbers to patterns. We can understand the rhythms of things by looking at the numeric equivalent of those rhythms. That is about as simple as I can make it, without losing the essence of what it is.

It might be easier if you imagine an electron going from point A to point B. It is constantly going in a motion, and it makes a fast beat or rhythm. It goes back and forth, point A to point B, thump and thump, in a rhythm. Let us say you could count it out to 13 beats a second, not to be precise because the timing is not as important as the number. The rhythm, 13 beats a second bouncing back and forth between point A and point B, creates a number due to its pattern. Every pattern has a number. Every pattern is a pattern because it is repetitious, and if it is repetitious, that means it is calculable.

Numbers and patterns create the galactic code. They are the language of the universe.

If everything has a pattern and if we could know all the variables acting on an object then, according to Chaos Theory, it would be possible to predict any pattern. Even the splashes of running water can be broken down into repetitious patterns. Because water keeps its pattern we can calculate how it is going to hit or fall. We could bounce a ball and while there may be a million variables acting on it, if we could know all of those variables, then the ball would follow the same pattern and become completely predictable.

That is a pretty startling and amazing thing if you think about it.

The universe, or this energy, God if you will, started to become aware of itself, its pattern. Collectively something came together. You see everything in the universe not only works in individual patterns but also as a collective pattern. Everything has a process that it contributes to, like a giant collective database. All of these little electrons, all these little things, had to accumulate to some pattern. They naturally sought out a purpose, it is evolution. It is natural within the laws of physics to create refined patterns, which in turn creates intelligence.

Let us look at this a different way and assume that complete chaos did exist. If it did exist, there would be no patterns. Everything would just be an infinite number of ever changing and truly unpredictable variables. If there were no patterns, there could be no variations of those patterns, and that means there would be no growth. Evolution requires patterns to refine and create variations from existing, stable ones. Because there was repetition and patterns, there could arise variations of those patterns. It could grow, evolve, and refine itself. However, that requires a consistent system from which to spring.

This energy, God, began to create variations of its pattern, which lead to the formation of its intelligence.

Over an unimaginably long period, God became intelligent as energy, as a giant form of prana. This energy was not uniform, is not uniform, and there are levels to it, many levels! We notate degrees of energy as levels of dimensions, which are completely separate realities.

For example, we refer to different levels of energy as the 3rd dimension or the 4th dimension. However, there are thousands of dimensions not just four or five. Imagine thousands of dimensions!

GOD EVOLVING THROUGH DIMENSIONS

Dimensions are the result of God creating variations of its own pattern.

As it creates variations of its own pattern, it moves its energy into other spaces creating new dimensions. We are not aware of them because we have to be moving at the rhythm or vibration of the energy that makes up each dimension. These other dimensions are things we can become aware of and experience using our energy bodies. We have to be able to learn to shift our consciousness to their frequency.

Here is an easy way to understand how dimensions work. Imagine you are standing by a highway. You are not doing anything, except looking at the road directly in front of you. At this moment, you are at the lowest frequency of energy.

Now while you are staring straight ahead with your sight fixed, a car drives past at 20 M.P.H. Are you going to be able to see very much of what was going on in the car? No. You have no idea what the driver looks like or what anyone in the car is doing. While you are staring straight at the middle of the road, zoom, the car passes in a blur. Then another car zips by even faster at 50 M.P.H., and you would be lucky to even know what the interior color of the car was. Then as you are still standing on the side of the road at the lowest frequency of energy another car goes by at 75 M.P.H and you can barely make out details about the car itself! Then one more car swooshes by even faster at 100 M.P.H., which from your perspective would be a blur. Each car passes at different speeds but each would be completely outside of your ability to clearly distinguish what may be occurring inside of each car.

Now imagine you jump into a car, accelerate to 50 M.P.H., and catch up to the car that passed you doing 20 M.P.H. You are no longer at the lowest frequency of energy. You are moving at a much faster rate than you were before but can you see inside of that car now? No, you pass it too quickly because now you are moving at a faster speed.

Can you see inside the car that is going 75 M.P.H? No, it is still traveling too fast for you to stay with it.

This is how dimensions work.

Dimensions are energy, vibration, or tonal. Now if your car is doing 50 M.P.H and another car merges onto the highway, pulls up next to you and it is doing 50 M.P.H, could you look over and see inside? Sure, you could. You could look over and see the driver fixing their hair, you could watch the passenger smacking their gum and throwing things at people in the backseat and everything going on inside the car. You are traveling at the same frequency. Everything around you right now, what you are sitting on, the book in your hand, you can experience because it is moving at the same rate or frequency as you. It is all the same dimension.

Different dimensions exist within the energy being, God, as higher and lower frequencies. As it created different things like molecules, electrons, different impulses, they all condensed into different forms of energy, at different speeds or rhythms of energy. Eventually it got down to a current that electrons would instantly solidify to become gases, much like water forming from condensation. Like raindrops that are so small but as they accumulate, they become heavy, they become water. Think of it as energy. The energy came to a point where it started to solidify and it became different kinds of gases, which were incoherent with one another.

Imagine an old wall clock, the kind with hands that move around in a circle. This clock will help illustrate a timeline in the creation of our universe. In the beginning both hands pointed straight up to 12, that is when God emerged in this dimension as a form of complex energy.

Once the clock ticks to the next minute that is when this giant gas cloud of energy ignited triggering an unbelievable explosion. Now imagine this explosion, beyond the size of 2,000 suns simultaneously going super nova. That is the Big Bang. The explosion is beyond enormous filling galaxies beyond galaxies of space with its energy.

After this explosion, we could say time has passed and the hand of the clock now ticks to five after. At this time, this energy, which has flooded the universe, changed from a super complex pure form of energy into a form of denser, less complex energy.

After the initial explosion, the high frequency energy began cooling and lowering in vibration. This denser energy then continued to slow and morphed and changed into progressively more dense forms of matter.

With each tick of the clock down from the twelve towards the six, or halfway through the hour, the energy that filled the universe morphed and became a denser energy as everything slowed down. This is only the progression of energy in our newly formed dimension, which is the universe we exist in now.

When the Big Bang happened energy from a higher dimension was sucked down into this one.

However, those higher variations of energy are still there and continue to exist within their appropriate dimension. When a new dimension is created energy from one dimension pushes into a new space, changing the pattern of that energy and creating another dimension.

The highest dimension is the frequency of God.

THE BIRTH OF THE UNIVERSE

This brings us back to the beginning of the universe when the energy that filled the universe ignited. However large you might be able to conceive an explosion it would probably be like saying that a flea sneezing was powerful and then compare that to 30 volcanoes erupting at the same time.

When it got to that point, between the energy and the molecule-like structures condensing the way they did, it created a super fusion explosion. As soon as this energy was released it was sucked out from the higher dimensions and instantly glued together certain ones that were attracted like magnets to specific other ones and quickly solidified creating matter. Matter solidified very quickly and that is when the explosion separated it all into a million infinitive directions.

This first explosion would become the basis for the eventual formation of all matter in this universe as it scattered in all directions. This would eventually evolve, over vast spans of time, into what we now know as planets, stars, solar systems, galaxies, and everything in the universe.

That was the creation of God, in this dimension.

That was the creation of matter and the universe as we experience it. I say it was the creation of God in this dimension because, as I have said, God exists in multiple dimensions. It is a multi-dimensional being.

This reality, our universe, is just one dimension. It is to say your finger is just a part of your whole body. This dimension is just a part, a finger, of God. If you could teleport to any location in the universe, no matter how far, you would still be in this dimension. Distance has no bearing on dimension because, no matter the distance, any location would still have the same frequency of energy.

That is what I mean when I say the Navigator is trying to lead us back to our higher consciousness, our dimensional consciousness. While many will relate to calling this part of us the higher consciousness, it is more accurate to call it our dimensional, or hyper-dimensional, consciousness. Now that we have discussed what dimensions are and how they work this term will make more sense. It is our energy consciousness that exists in a higher frequency of energy, a separate dimensional state.

Our true self exists in a hyper-dimensional state.

This true self, our true consciousness, the part of us that is timeless, eternal and stores the collective memories of all our past lives is our hyper-dimensional consciousness. Let us take a moment and closely look at what this term means.

'Dimensional' means that this consciousness operates on a different frequency than our immediate waking consciousness. We must go through the process of raising our tonal and frequency to connect to it. 'Hyper' implies that we are not talking about a minor shift in dimensional frequency; it is super fast, a very high frequency of energy, which is very close to the tonal of the Force. 'Consciousness' says that it has an awareness all its own.

That means it exists at a super high-vibration, dimensional place. The tonal of the Force, the very source of everything, exists at the highest dimensional frequency.

The more we raise our consciousness, which is energy, the closer we come to the frequency of the Force, and the closer we come to awakening.

Considering the journey we have been on you may find yourself asking, why? Not why does the process of awakening exist, though you may ask that as well, but why is the Force doing this? Why evolve, why create variations of its own pattern? It is true that I have told you the how of its coming to be, not the why.

These are important questions. In these questions lie many mysteries. Let us continue our journey of discovery to uncover the answers. You may find that in understanding the reason and purpose of the Universe you begin to realize the very reason and purpose for your own being

CHAPTER FIVE

UNVEILING THE
UNIVERSAL PURPOSE

Unveiling the Universal Purpose

An in-between place that defies logic as humanity understands it.

You exist in more than one dimension. Your being is multi-dimensional. I want you to think about what that means for a moment. Recite the alphabet right now. Where do you experience the familiar sing-song sequence of letters? If you are like most people, you hear it, or say it, in your head.

The letters exist in your head.

Right now when you think about the letters, they exist in your mind. Even if you were to write the letters on a piece of paper your only knowledge of that paper will come to you through your senses and exist in your mind. We often identify our physical bodies as the center of our being because they are easily identifiable things that we control. We experience pain, pleasure, all of our emotions and senses through the body but is it really who we are?

If you cut off your arm, is the arm still you? Or do you identify it as a functioning part of your body? We use it as a tool. As we experience, the body converts all of the things we experience into energy. The mind interprets all of the data from our senses into energy. Our true being, what we really are, is composed of energy, our memories are energy, and our experiences are energy.

We are energy beings.

HOW ENERGY EXPERIENCES

The physical body is like an All Terrain Vehicle for our energy being or dimensional consciousness. Rather than thinking of the dimensional consciousness as a collection of thoughts floating without form, it is easier if you look at it as a separate being, which is what it is. This separate energy being uses the body to move around and gather experiences.

Imagine a cup of water sitting on a small table next to you. Now suddenly you realize that your body is thirsty so you command your body to reach out and take the cup. You raise the cup with practiced precision from the table, bring it to the mouth, take a sip, taste the water and return the cup to the table. You can perform this process almost without effort. Consider how many separate actions your body executed to perform this simple task, yet it takes very little thought on your part. Thoughts direct the body, which responds like a perfect automated machine by reaching out and taking a sip.

The body is our method of transportation. It allows us to move through this space or dimension. It also gathers experiences for us as we move around. How does it do this? It does this by converting physical experience into energy.

The brain converts everything that we touch into energy. It converts everything that we hear into energy. It converts everything that we see into energy. It converts everything that we taste into energy.

All of the senses receive information from this dimension and convert that information into impulses of energy or electricity. Do you understand? Have you ever wondered why? Have you ever marveled at the process of it? This is so that we, as dimensional energy beings, can consume this energy and in doing so become aware of it.

We are energy beings residing in bodies so that we can experience this physical dimension.

The relationship between our energy being and our physical body is kind of like a person driving a car, except imagine that the person driving believes the car is their true being. It might strike you as funny to imagine a person who believes that they are the car, but that is the way most of us think of ourselves. We do not separate our physical bodies from the pure energy being that controls the body. When people drive cars, they do not become car-beings.

We are the energy beings within our bodies.

We are not really the physical body, but an energy being that is manipulating the body and experiencing through it. Think again of driving a car. While driving, our body is manipulating a set of controls to produce a desired result. The car is a tool that we are using in order to do something that we cannot do with our body alone. Usually what we want is to get, quickly, from one place to another.

While driving, are we the car?

No, the car remains the car and we remain who we are. Yet, if we hit bumps in the road do we not experience it with the car? If we turn quickly, do we not grab onto the handle and feel the force of the turn? What is more, even though the car is taking us where we want to go are we not absorbing the experience as we see the sights?

There is a similar connection between the physical body and energy body. There is a relationship between the two but the two remain independent of each other. Cars are designed to be operated by human bodies but humans still have to spend considerable time learning how to use them.

In the same way that our physical body uses the car as a tool to transport it from one place to another, the real us, the energy being, uses the body as a tool to help it experience and do things that is not capable of doing as pure energy.

Just as it took our body some time to learn how to drive a car it also took us some time to learn how to use the body. It can take us years to even develop basic talking and walking skills. We are energy beings using physical organic bodies as tools.

Our true being exists in another dimension and it partakes of and infuses with this dimension using bodies. Our bodies are constructs of this dimension that allow us to experience it.

Now, if we use our bodies to gather information and then convert that information into energy so that our energy being can have experiences, does God work in a similar way? Yes, once again we can see the reflection of micro-life mirrored in the macro.

The Universe is the body of God. Everything in the Universe will eventually change back into pure energy. The question is, if the Universe is converting back into energy then where is that energy going?

Does that body, the Universe or God, have a consciousness?

A QUESTION OF CONSCIOUSNESS

God does have a consciousness but not the kind that we might imagine. The consciousness of God is so different from our consciousness that it is almost entirely outside of our ability to even conceive it. You might as well say it does not have a consciousness just to understand how truly different it is than ours. There is no comparison.

Right now, imagine that we are searching for the consciousness of a snail or a slug, or an ant. We may not be able to know what they are thinking but we can imagine what motivates them. We are able to come to terms with what their existence must be like so we have a starting point for imagining their awareness. We can imagine what the consciousness of these bugs might be like because we can observe them. We are the observers, we look at them, we have watched educational programs or science shows so we have some basic knowledge of how they function.

Now consider the opposite end of the spectrum.

Instead of imagining the awareness of something smaller than we are, imagine the consciousness of something much larger. Think about what it would be like for the ant, whose mind we were just trying to understand, to conceive of what we are and what our consciousness is like. It might as well consider us a geographical feature we are so much larger than it is! For it to understand how our minds work, and what we think, it would have to understand the concepts that we all share.

The ant would have to understand our laws, fashions, civilizations, nations, or even our giant sprawling cities. It would be impossible! How could an ant comprehend such things?

Even the idea of everything involved in creating this simple book would be far beyond this tiny little insect's ability to conceive! It is no different for us to attempt to conceive the mind of God. It is a difficult thing for us to do. After all, we have only just begun to explore our solar system. Humans have only reached the moon, which is hardly a step compared to the size of the universe.

The scale of the being that we are trying to consider renders it inconceivable to us.

Forget the ant trying to conceive a human, think about it trying to visualize a planet or even a solar system. This barely approaches the scale of us trying to understand the mind of the Universe and the workings of God. Even describing the physical nature of such a being is extremely difficult. Describing the thoughts of that being borders on impossible.

To illustrate the scale of this creature, imagine that you are standing on a beach. Now bend down and pick up a single grain of sand, that single grain will represent our solar system. The entire solar system is inside of that single grain of sand! Now look down, underneath your feet and all around you. There is an entire beach of sand. You cannot even see the whole beach because it disappears over the horizon. Thinking about our solar system as a single grain of sand will begin to give you an idea of how incredibly vast our universe is.

Now, we can discuss the truth of how God thinks but it is a bit tricky.

THE MIND OF GOD

Our brains tell our hearts to pump and keep our livers, kidneys and other organs functioning by sending out signals or sensory impulses. Most of us are completely unaware of our bodies as they function on this level.

Think about it, when was the last time you had to sit there and think, 'Okay heart keep beating and stomach don't stop digesting that snack I just ate and oops, I haven't told my liver to function in 20 minutes, that's going to hurt.' We do not have to do that because our brain automatically tells our body how to function through something like low-radiation or electrical impulses. The only time we might become aware of how our body is functioning is when we have a problem, like a stomachache.

We can become aware of our body and master all kinds of functions. There are yogis who can control their bodies in amazing ways. These individuals have tapped into their deep inner consciousness. They are utilizing an inner-verse, a different dimension of their body. As we ponder the different levels on which our bodies function, many questions form. If our bodies function without our direct awareness then does the Universe have a similar mechanism?

Solar radiation manipulates, to some degree, our species. You see, all the stars in the universe are like the neo-synapses of the brain. Our brain releases sparks of information, or data, that moves across the expanses of our brain to other parts or points that reciprocate. Just as our neo-synapses perform this function for our brain, all the stars in the universe do the same through light.

The stars emit solar radiation in millions of frequencies, which are constantly hitting the planet and everything in it. Like a giant orchestra playing its rhythm upon a small ball. All these different pitches and frequencies constantly affect us. Because we and every creature on this planet are electrical beings, we are receptive to this manipulation. It affects our societies as if they were giant organisms moving on the planet.

So God, or the Force, is communicating through the stars, through solar radiation, in much the way our brain communicates with our body. It happens without us realizing that the electrons in our brain are manipulating other electrons.

In this process, God communicates using solar radiation as our brains use impulse radiation. God communicates with different planets, solar systems, and galaxies in the same way our brains communicate with our separate organs. Just as all of our body's organs are different and serve special functions, so these 'organs' within the body of God are also very different and serve special functions.

That is one way God thinks or communicates to its body, the Universe. It uses solar radiation.

We must also understand that God is more like an organism than a thing with intent. It does not necessarily have a distinct plan for the Earth and certainly, it does not have a specific plan for each individual.

God is aware of us in the way that we are aware of our hand or our thumb.

We are protective of our body, we use it, but we do not directly think about all the individual organisms inside of it. We simply see it as a thing to use. If something happens to our body, we react, if it is in danger we feel the alarm that is emanating from millions of cells saying, 'Hey, help us!' God might have a similar reaction if the planet was in danger. Our collective consciousness would reach out, God would feel a tiny pinprick in say the palm of the Universe, and it might go to metaphorically scratch it.

We cannot easily identify, on our level of existence, the kind of awareness that God has. Right now, we are not aware of our kidneys or our liver but they are functioning. There is no awareness unless we feel pain, unless we feel death. In this same way, God is not aware of every minute detail but it is aware of great imbalances.

Because we are a part of God if something were to happen to the human race, we would collectively reach out and catch, in a sense, God's attention. That attention would manifest and focus on us through the Force in the same way our consciousness focuses on an area of our body that reports having trouble. Our true essence is the energy being that resides in our physical body. God is energy, and its body, its flesh and blood, is the planets and the stars.

God's soul, the Force, intertwines with its body in the same way that our minds intertwine with our bodies.

If we examine life on our planet, we can see signs of how this consciousness manifests. There are clues of its awareness and subtle manipulations created from its attention.

Let us look at some insects for practical examples of this intelligence. Insects have amazing social systems to relay information. One ant will run into another one, they will touch antennae, exchange data, and keep moving. Do ants collectively make progress as individuals die? Ants probably make no visible progress collectively on the scale of a few generations. However, ants will become much smarter collectively over the course of millions of years. Is this a result of the ants sharing information or is there some other way that they change and become smarter collectively?

THE AWARENESS BEHIND REALITY

Consider the researched and documented case of the Owl Butterfly. The Owl Butterfly lives in rainforests, from Mexico to Brazil. Birds are the natural predators of the Owl Butterfly. The predators of these birds are owls that live in the same rainforests as the birds and the Owl Butterfly.

Like all owls, these owls have very distinctive colored markings around their eyes unique to their species, and birds recognize their predator, the owl, by these distinctive markings. When a bird sees the eye of an owl, its brain registers that it is in danger and it should fly away. Now these birds prey on a very specific butterfly, aptly named the Owl Butterfly. This butterfly is a main meal for these birds.

Somehow, this butterfly, which as far as we are concerned has below zero intelligence, has a wing pattern, which is identical to the color and pattern of the owl's eyes. When the butterfly extends its wings, it reveals the pattern matching the owl's eyes. The bird recognizes the pattern, on the butterfly's wing, as the eye of its feared predator, panics and leaves. If the bird spies the butterfly, but does not recognize the pattern on the butterfly's wing, then it has a tasty treat. This maintains an amazing balance in the butterfly population and in the ecosystem as a whole.

Are we to believe that this is pure coincidence?

Did all of these butterflies get together and decide, "Hey! Let's get together and wear this owl's eye!" Why that owl when there are hundreds to choose from? To get that specific owl and that particular pattern is astonishing.

We could say it is a progression of genes or genetics but even these concepts must have data reported to them somehow. Somewhere a connection formed between the owls, birds, and butterflies.

In human evolution, we think of an ape-man slowly becoming erect and over time becoming smarter and more adept. Our evolution allowed us to shape our reality by creating tools and technology. Did the butterfly follow the same evolutionary path? Did its intelligence increase over time? Did it knowingly shape its reality by matching its markings to an owl? No way.

Did the butterfly, at any point, understand the distinguishing mark of a specific owl? Was it ever knowingly conscious of it or possess the ability to willfully modify its own wing pattern? It could not know what specific pattern on a particular kind of owl would do the trick. The butterfly possesses no means of deducing that kind of information. The random mutation that powers evolution cannot explain what happened.

Something was at work that was more intricate than evolution.

The result shows that it is beyond a random force of nature to create such a specific solution. It is also beyond Darwin's theory of Natural Selection. Simply put, the theory states that there could have been hundreds of kinds of butterflies and over thousands of years they were reduced to the most successful species. The strongest and most suited for the environment was the one that survived hence the Owl Butterfly. Natural Selection has some truth to it but it is part of the automation. It is like the difference between our body functioning automatically and willful, conscious intervention.

Something wanted a progression of life and collected all this environmental data to make a willful intervention. This something knew that the bird fed on the butterfly and that the owl was the bird's natural predator. It also knew that it needed the Owl Butterfly to pollinate fruit trees. The Owl Butterfly would get pollen on its back and travel among the trees pollinating them because the butterfly was attracted to the flowers.

It also knew that when the fruits of these trees were pollinated it needed this specific bird, which was inclined to eat these seeds, to eat and digest them and then spread them around so they would get planted and grow elsewhere. It knew it needed this bird but it had to weigh things out. It needed a balance. It needed to control the birds, the owls and the butterflies so it created this natural ecosystem. Humans certainly did not do that. We had no part in creating that system.

This is where the elusive answer to the problem is. The butterfly's wing is a clue of some greater presence or intelligence at work.

It specifically made the wing pattern the same as the eye of the owl. This way, half the time when the bird flies down for lunch and it cannot see the butterfly's wing, the bird eats the butterfly. The other fifty percent of the time the butterfly turns sideways and the bird is frightened off. This ensures that the butterfly survives and maintains the balance in the ecosystem. An intelligence intervened to ensure the balance and survival of this ecosystem.

This intelligence was the Gaia consciousness, the consciousness of the planet, working on an amazingly complex level. Nothing other than a consciousness could have been so specific. The only other option would be divine intervention. That would be a direct intervention by the Force subtly influencing reality.

However, if our planet, Gaia, has a consciousness and can influence physical reality then the Universe is certainly capable of a similar intervention. The case of the Owl Butterfly is one of many which show that the Force is constantly here and demonstrates how the Force works on very subtle levels.

The example of the Owl Butterfly shows that Gaia, which is a very complex living organism, and ultimately the Universe, have a level of self-awareness and demonstrates how this awareness manifests itself in our reality.

This or similar interventions are the Force trying to preserve the existence and growth of life. It must do this in subtle and delicate ways. Everything in the Universe is struggling to survive. Life wants to evolve.

This is what every planet in the universe does. It is what every living thing does. It is part of the divine process.

THE DIVINE PROCESS

All of this ties into one of the great secrets. This is the kind of secret that in order to find an answer, a person has to travel thousands of miles, crawl up the side of the highest peak of a brutal, snow-covered, wind-swept mountain range to find a half-starved blind yogi. Although we are not going to go through all of that, we will ask the question and search for its answer. That is right, what is the meaning of life?

Everybody asks this question almost without fail. I could write the meaning of life on the back of a fortune cookie but the explanation of the answer could take years to unravel and see the truth of it.

The meaning of life is to experience.

We are energy beings in physical bodies in this dimension to experience what we could not as pure energy. As energy we do not have nasal glands so we cannot smell, we do not have ear drums so we cannot hear, we cannot see because we have no eyes, we cannot taste because we have no taste buds and we cannot touch! As an energy being, this whole universe of matter does not exist. This dimension is like a smorgasbord of experiences.

For an energy being, our world is like being a seven year old at Disneyland!

It is a magical wonderland! We can experience things with this body that are new, exciting and unexpected! Our bodies transform and interpret data, or experiences, into energy so they can become part of our consciousness.

This is what I mean when I say the meaning of life is to experience. It is to experience the sun on our faces, it is to feel the moisture of wet dewy grass on our toes, it is to feel the wind in our hair, and it is to hear birds sing. It is to kiss, to hug and it is to roll around in the dirt and taste the dust in our mouths! It is to laugh!

The meaning of life is to experience and do all of the things that we cannot do as energy beings.

Existing as an energy being is not a bad thing, but it is so very different from this existence. This existence is to be imagined, to be tasted, to be enlivened. To not experience or to suppress another from experiencing is one of the few truly great universal wrongs.

Everything that is living has a natural desire to live. Even animals far below human intelligence do not just run off cliffs. Everything has a sense of life. Everything wants to live because infused in everything is the Force, and its energy tells us to live. This same energy functions to protect the planet, the solar system, the galaxy, the universe and ultimately the consciousness of God.

We are also infused with energy, which we have been talking

about. While we cannot experience this dimension with our energy bodies, we can share our experiences and pass them on through our energy.

Look at how our experiences are created and transformed. Everything we see, smell, touch, taste, or hear is converted into electricity. Every experience in life arrives to our being in the form of electrical impulses. Every experience that we receive happens because the cells of our bodies share copies of their experiences by sending electrical impulses on to the brain and eventually surrender their existence for our experience. While 'we' the being will live for many years to come, the cells within our inner-universe, our body, will die and be replaced constantly throughout our life.

Now pause for a moment and look around the room. Maybe you are resting comfortably in a soft chair, or a leather couch, or at a hard table drinking coffee. Reach out with your hand and feel the things that are around you. Perhaps you feel the softness of the chair or a smooth cup that is warm from the drink it contains. To have this simple experience of touch, tiny electrical signals are fired through your nervous system and the brain registers them. However, 'you' did not actually have that experience. Micro individual cells shared the feeling of touch so that 'you' could experience that moment.

You live through their experiences.

What will be a very brief moment of your total life will be a lifetime for all of the micro life that makes up your physical body. The consciousness, if you could call it that, of each cell is like a raindrop. When they are all collected in a bucket, that water is your consciousness.

When we look back on these collected experiences, like data stored on a computer chip, we recall all of them as energy. Because every experience we have is converted from our nervous system into energy, it is also stored and recalled as energy from our electrical bodies. This is why modern science does not know where memories are stored in the brain. It is known that chemical releases signal memories being triggered but it is not known where they come from.

They are stored as energy separate from the physical brain.

When most people die this energy, their stored consciousness and the totality of who they are, is absorbed into the collective consciousness of the Earth. Much like the cells of our body, when they die and their electrical essence contributes to you, so do beings on this planet contribute to the Earth's consciousness.

This is how the Earth grows and experiences.

Earlier when you touched an object close to you, the cells of your body shared their experience with you allowing you to feel the world around you. In a sense, they willingly surrender their existence to you, as lifetimes of cells pass in a very short period of your life.

A moment for you can be a lifetime for your cells.

I told you before that viewing the life of a cell as short was just a matter of perspective. That is what it is here as well. A human lifetime seems like a very long period for us but for the Earth it is only a brief moment. The scale of an experience is relative to the perspective that one takes when viewing the experience. Relationships between things on large and small scales reflect each other. A process that occurs on a very micro level can often be seen occurring in a similar way on a very macro level.

We will live our lives, from a few moments to a hundred years, only to give up our existence and memories to the planet.

The planet, which is just a tiny microbe compared to the universe, will live for billions of years and then surrender its entire experience, its consciousness, to the solar system. It will pass its experiences on by surrendering its consciousness. The planet is part of a larger system that will contribute to a greater being, just as the individual cells in our bodies do for us.

In time, even the solar system will give all of its data to our galaxy, and the galaxies will give their data to the universe, which is the body of God. The entire universe is going through this process from the extremely micro to the vastly inconceivably macro.

At the point where all things rejoin the body of God, everything becomes energy.

Over a long time, longer than any human brain could imagine, the universe, which began as pure energy and then slowed to denser forms of matter, will again accelerate to pure energy. God will then receive this energy in the form of an experience.

From our perspective an almost infinite amount of time will pass.

The entire existence of this universe will morph, evolve and then give up its life to God. All so God can take a sip of its tea, per se, smile and say, "oh, so that is what that was, how wonderful". It will experience that moment, all of those collected experiences, in a single moment.

We receive all of our experiences after they are converted into energy and so does everything, from our planet, the galaxy, the Universe and then on to God. Everything receives experiences after they are transported through physical beings and changed into energy.

God wants to experience, live, and know what it does not already know.

It is only our perspective that limits our understanding of God. That is what separates us. A hundred billion micro-moments make up our experiences. God's experiences consist of the same moments but on a vastly different scale. Size alone should not be a reason to measure an experience as significant or insignificant. We cannot discount an experience because it seems so small, or so short a moment. It is by no means insignificant.

Without the lives of our micro-cells, we would experience nothing.

Without the sensation of every touch, or smell, every taste and sound, we would experience nothing. All of these things make it what it is. Even if the existence of our entire universe is but the shortest moment for God, it is a moment of invaluable importance, of immeasurable possibility. Everything within that moment, no matter the size, contributes to that.

What is more beautiful or precious than that? Yet, it is all so fragile.

We have many obstacles in life. There are many risks and dangers along the way. The Universe faces its own dangers. The purpose of White Cells is to protect and preserve life. If the Force is all that there is and it pushes everything to live and grow then what is the reason for white cells? We spoke earlier about defending the planet, defending life, against things similar to viruses. Our Universe, the experience of God, is not all that there is. There is another force. It is as present and active as the Force so it is just as necessary to discuss.

CHAPTER SIX

THE REACTION OF CREATION

THE REACTION OF CREATION

Your hidden senses tell you, that what your eyes see, and hands touch, is not all that there is.

The Force emerged in this dimension creating the Universe. It emerged with an explosion of such power and magnitude it is beyond imagining. God now exists, grows, and wills all life to experience. God desires.

It desires to know and to experience all that it does not already know but something opposes that desire.

The laws of physics state that in this universe, for every action there is an opposite reaction. With so much energy and force involved in the creation of this dimension there would have to be some kind of reaction. The reaction to the amazing force that emerged along with the creation of matter is the opposite of everything that God created. It is the 'Darkside'.

We could call it evil but it is more accurate to call it anti-matter, or anti-life. The 'Darkside' is the negative of God. It is pushing the Universe to return to the nothing that existed before God.

CLASHING FORCES: THE EXISTENCE OF ANTI-MATTER

The Darkside is the opposing force of life, the stars, the planets and the Universe itself. This concept should not be difficult or unexpected to most people. Instinctually, most of us are aware of a hidden consciousness behind life and we are often equally aware of an opposing force.

The challenge before us is to knowingly admit that God wants us to live and experience life but that this experience is not certain. It is more difficult than one might think to look around at life and accept the possibility that its existence has no guarantee. With this done, we must also seek out a reason for why there is a Darkside. Understand that there is a positive force of energy, which is what we are a part of, and there is an opposing force, which is the origin of our concept of evil.

This concept of evil is different from our concepts of morality and ethics. This is important to discuss because the moment I say evil many misconceptions may fill your thoughts. As with many of the things I discuss, if you cannot recognize and acknowledge something, you can do nothing with it, or in this case, against it. The nature of anti-matter is as subtle and elusive as the workings of the Force, so we must analyze what it is and what it is not.

It is important not to mix morality or ethics with the workings of the Darkside. Stealing a car, for example, might be immoral and unethical, which are rules created and determined by a society, but it is not a truly evil act. What is evil is the suppression or killing of life.

If one were to kidnap a person and suppress them by locking them in a room and deprive them of the sensations of new things or experiences, that is the Darkside. That is evil.

To abuse someone and fill them with fear of living life, of going out and experiencing all that life has to offer, is evil. To kill life is wrong. Now granted we could have a detailed discussion about whether or not it is wrong to eat meat, cut down trees or anything else like that, but for now let us agree that in general it is wrong to kill, destroy, or desire to harm *human* life.

To mentally torture, or make someone have suppressive feelings and turn them into a recluse is an act of evil because these things are against the purpose of life, which is to experience! The Darkside wants to eradicate life. Any act that serves the purpose of limiting or ending life is the only thing that is truly evil. Acts that limit or end life serve the will of the Darkside.

Anything that flourishes with life is an opposing force to the Darkside.

The expanding Universe opposes the Darkside, which wants to return to nothing. The two are in conflict, the Darkside wants to squash the Universe and make it disappear.

The Darkside is a reaction, an opposing force.

Anything that promotes life also attracts the Darkside, which will oppose its growth. Both the forces of God and the Darkside exist everywhere. The relationship of the Darkside and God is like oil and vinegar. We can look at oil and vinegar in a still bottle and they will be separate with one floating on top of the other. When we shake that bottle, it will look like one pinkish fluid. The two fluids are still separate but they are so tiny that we cannot tell by casually looking. If we look closely, we see the little oil dots and bubbles of vinegar.

This is similar to the energy of the Force and the Darkside. Both kinds of energy are everywhere.

Whatever we attract is what we will consume, as energy, and utilize in a positive way or a negative way. Although the Darkside dislikes humanity, it is not unlike the Darkside to utilize or empower someone to unleash destruction in this dimension. As the Darkside is as present as the Force, it can also be as influential. It sees life as a tool. The Darkside can manipulate some people to create death and destruction.

THE MANIPULATION OF LIFE

The reason the Darkside is interested in the Earth is quite simple; Earth is a source of life.

If the Earth is a living organism, then every planet in the universe is also alive. Maybe in some ways they are not as advanced as the Earth, in other ways they might be more advanced. As the Earth changes and evolves and life grows and becomes more intelligent, the interest of the Darkside grows.

As humanity develops the Earth and the Force grows stronger with us, the Darkside will continue to accumulate and attempt to find points that it can crack into, to somehow eradicate or spoil this process.

The process that it wants to stop is our continued development of the planet.

People may say that the growing human population is bad, that we are like a disease on the planet. This is not true. Certainly, some of the things that humanity does to the Earth are bad and it is important for us to protect and use the planet's resources wisely. Nevertheless, it is our mission to collectively evolve this planet.

We are supposed to change the planet from what it was, into some other, more evolved form. The Earth has a purpose, a divine plan of sorts, which is the real threat to the Darkside. Humanity plays a pivotal role in this plan. The plan involves humanity as it fashions a higher functioning for this planet.

We are enabling the planet to expand beyond its current boundaries.

By creating satellites and moving our intelligence off the planet, we are extending the reach of the planetary organism that is Gaia. The planet is expanding by using its collective resources to evolve. It has its own way of creating its sensory and it uses mankind as a part of that sensory. This is a normal process.

Think about what we have discussed about using our body to collect data and experiences for our energy consciousness. Look at your arm and think about what it does. It reaches out beyond the boundary of your main torso and touches the world around you. It collects data. Do you recall our discussion about how not all beings need arms and legs to be alive? The planet does not have arms to reach out so it will use us to create spacecraft, satellites and all kinds of other technologies to move beyond its own boundaries and touch the universe around it.

We will bring these experiences back and surrender them to Gaia so that it can learn and grow.

Consider the human brain, which has three layers to it. There is a reptilian center, a mammalian inner-layer and the outer neo-cortex. Over time, the human species evolved and became more complex which allowed us to shape the planet in new and fascinating ways. Gaia is no different with how it will shape the universe as it grows and learns.

The planet, which is an evolving life form, is becoming more alive. It is getting older and more advanced and finding its form.

The Darkside does not want the Earth to evolve and mature because that means eventually, much like all things on this planet, it will procreate. It will create more of itself, just as every species on our planet multiplies so too will this planet reproduce. It will not procreate as humans do, as it is more of a hermaphrodite, like a worm that has qualities of both male and female. If you consider how trees spawn and spread then the idea of Earth procreating will not seem so very strange.

It will use us, like a bee pollinating flowers, and we will go to the stars.

We will create spacecraft and we will pollinate the moon, and Mars and we will create life in these places. We will take the DNA of the Earth to other planets. We will take the DNA of fruit and trees to grow. We will create water and an atmosphere to allow life to flourish, thus mimicking our planet repeatedly throughout the universe.

It may take us a hundred years to begin to accomplish this next evolutionary step but that is not a long time for the planet. From our point of view a hundred years might seem like a long time, but to a planet that is billions of years old, a hundred years will pass like a moment. However long it takes, the next evolutionary step is an important one. The planet is a living organism and its purpose is to procreate and expand. As it feels that desire, it is reflected in us.

As a species, we know, instinctually, that our purpose is to go to the stars.

Most of us crave to go into the universe because it is the destiny of humanity. Our souls came from a place of knowledge so that we are able to inform the rest of the world. The role of an enlightened person is to communicate the knowledge of their dimensional consciousness to the rest of the world. These people are the White Cells from our previous analogy.

When one of these individuals becomes very spiritually advanced, they will be able to feel the rhythm of the life of the planet. They are here to preserve the life of the planet and to keep it healthy so it can continue to grow. The purpose of a White Cell is to oppose the Darkside and promote life on the Earth. The Darkside opposes this expansion and advancing of life. It wants to hold us back to prevent this from happening.

It opposes us because it sees that this is our purpose.

Understand that I simplify my explanations and analogies of the Darkside, White Cells, and the Force in many ways. For the sake of clearly communicating these concepts, I have tried to explain these things in very basic terms. This knowledge must be able to reach every person who is seeking it. If someone feels compelled to read this book and does not understand what I am talking about, my efforts would be for nothing. What is the use of explaining anything if only a select few can understand it?

Many people will read this description and think it all sounds too much like a movie. They will intellectually dismiss it because it sounds too cut and dried or black and white. They will tell themselves the world is more complicated than that. Well, yes and no. The world is more complicated, but consider why we need white cells in our bodies. With outside influences such as viruses and diseases that interfere with our inner universe, we require their existence.

White cells exist in our bodies because there is a need for them.

If there is a need for cells to counter life-threatening influences in our bodies, it makes sense that larger organisms, such as the planet, have a similar need. Our small-scale perspective limits our ability to see the large-scale reflection. We dismiss that it could ever be broken down so simply as two opposing forces. While it may be as simple as two opposing forces, how those forces play out and the nature of how they have woven into the fabric of reality in this dimension is not simple. Nothing in this world is as simple as the analogies that I employ to explain it. However, do not overlook the simple reality that two opposing forces are continuing a complicated struggle in this dimension.

There is a danger in dismissing the basic reality of the Darkside.

If we discard it as an immature concept, we limit our ability to move with the Force. A person cannot stumble onto a path of enlightenment, it will take deliberate effort to understand and align oneself with the Force. That is the ultimate goal of enlightenment after all, to align oneself with the Force. If you deny the existence of the Darkside then you do not accept the Force. If you do not accept the Force, you will never awaken.

Many have fallen into this trap.

WHEN NON-DUALITY BECOMES NEUTRALITY

A growing number of people seek what they perceive to be a more direct spiritual path. Many of these people adopt a misinterpretation of the concept of oneness or non-duality. Oneness or non-duality means that there is no duality; the Force and the Darkside are really one thing. There are many different variations and interpretations of this philosophy but for the sake of this argument, I will simply state part of this belief is that the ultimate nature of everything is happening just as it should.

It suggests that who you think you are is an illusion and that if you believe you have a choice you are simply playing along with the illusion of your ego. It implies that any choice you make is not truly a choice. Instead, your choices are nothing but a combination of reactions resulting from a series of causes that preceded them.

In other words, the whole universe from the very beginning has been nothing more than an amazingly elaborate series of causes and effects.

Adopting this, one can be led to accept that they are no longer truly responsible for their choices and that everything is happening as it should.

While parts of this philosophy hold great truth, the danger is that it can lead you into a state of non-action. It puts your consciousness in a loop. The helpless belief that your choices will not affect your journey to awakening subdues your natural urge to grow your consciousness. If a person adopts this as ultimate truth, one question always seems to arise, what does it matter what choice I make?

An immature non-dualist point of view could look at the Force and the Darkside and reduce them to mere concepts and part of the illusion.

The universe is unfolding as it should, so why bother making a choice when everything is working perfectly as is? The truth is, yes, there is a cause and effect nature to the universe, its beginning was God bursting into this dimension and forming the present duality. This does not mean you should act from a perspective based upon that level.

Living your life by that 'big picture' philosophy can result in the inability to make decisions that would allow you to expand and grow your consciousness. Will leading your life by the faith that everything is occurring as it should lead you to awakening? No. If choices are illusions of the ego, will the inability to act decisively actually neuter your spiritual development? Yes. It will also lessen your opportunity to tap into the force, which will deny you entrance into any level of enlightenment and ensure you will never fulfill your higher purpose.

In this dimension, everything has an opposite; one aspect cannot exist without the other.

Therefore, they must both exist to define the greater whole; light cannot exist without darkness or good cannot exist without evil and life defines death. Reflect back on our discussion about the creation of the Universe and the varying dimensions of God.

When God created this dimension, the entire Universe, it did so by moving its energy into this place from a higher dimension. Remember that God grows and evolves by creating variations of its own energy. The higher dimension where God moved its energy from is still there. There are even higher dimensions beyond that.

All of these dimensions of God exist without the Darkside.

This philosophy has failed because it does not recognize God exists in dimensions without the Darkside. God *encountered* the Darkside in this dimension. God would still exist even if the Darkside were not here! The Darkside is here and so is God. We, are a part of God. That is the nature of the struggle of our Universe.

Those who fall into the belief that reduces the forces of dark and light into facets of a much bigger picture will have cheated themselves. This reduction allows them to accept both. They will never awaken to higher dimensions where only the Force exists.

Do you see the trap?

They must accept them both because in this belief the Darkside is essential for God to exist. The fact is that as long as a person holds this kind of misinterpretation of non-dualistic belief they will never know the Force because they will have turned away from it.

It is true that in this Universe when God entered this dimension, there was a reaction and that reaction was anti-matter. To suggest that the Force cannot exist apart from anti-matter is to become blind to the struggle that is life. All life could cease. The Darkside could wipe out all life in this Universe and end this grand experience of which we are all a part.

Life and our planet are very precious because they are fragile.

The Universe is dancing away consumed in the experiences of life and anti-matter is burning like a fire all around God waiting to engulf everything. When we touch something, our cells give us a carbon copy of its experience. Cells transform the moment into electricity, so that we can know what it is to feel. Everything in this Universe must also transform back into energy in order for God to experience it. We cannot know an experience, icy cold snow or warm sand from a beach, until that electrical signal travels to our brain and we live it.

God cannot know the full experience of this Universe until it all evolves, or converts, into energy and travels back to God.

At any moment and at any time anti-matter could disrupt the whole process and all could truly be lost. There is no guarantee enforcing the balance between the Force and the Darkside. The Darkside could destroy all life in the Universe and this part of God would die with it. Do you not see the preciousness of this?

However very real the dangers to the Universe might be, we remain free to choose to be oblivious, or to help the Universe. God is curious and wants to experience everything. It cannot do this if we are tightly bound to its will and forced to serve it. Such structure and control is a trait of the Darkside not the Force. We must be free to explore and experience all that we choose if the Universe is to continue its process of evolution.

It is important to accept and serve the Force because it is our choice to make, and not everyone will.

As the Force is to the Universe, electrically we are the spirit, or the force of the micro-verse of our body. Our micro-verse succumbs to our will. If our energy being becomes depressed, this affects our body and it may hinder how well it functions. If our energy being is feeling positive, our body can benefit. Now God does not have simple emotions, like we do, but there is a sense of energy that we are receptive to and it can affect us.

We can also choose to tap this energy and do amazing, powerful things with it, if we know how. Call it tapping the Force, the power of the Force, call it what you like. There are stories of people who have done amazing, miraculous things and display incredible mystical powers when they surrender to the will of the Force.

These stories have truth to them. There are ways to do the things that they describe.

There is a way to tap the Force and consume this energy. We can change our tonal, the vibration of our consciousness, like a tuning fork. God is at a very high vibration and we exist on a much lower vibration or dimension. You could say we are moving at 10 M.P.H, and God in the higher dimension is zipping along going 75 or 100. If we raise our frequency to match these speeds we can be like the car driving next to the other car and see what is going on inside. When we raise our tonal close to say, 75 or 100 M.P.H, we can conceive of and become a vibration with God.

That is enlightenment.

When we achieve a state of enlightenment we continue to act in this dimension but use knowledge or power from a much higher dimension. To achieve enlightenment we must seek and apply effort to move our consciousness to the vibration of the Force. When this happens we are, in a sense, one with the Universe and God. For this to happen we must surrender and open our total being to the Force, only then can it channel through us.

Can you imagine if the next time you caught a simple cold, all of your white cells sat down and said, 'Oh well, it's all happening as it should so we should accept it all,' and then did nothing?

You would die.

On your death bed you would be fighting to survive, remembering all the moments of your life from laughter with loved ones, to time spent with friends, all of your greatest achievements and bitterest defeats. Chances are you would not be ready to give it up. You would want to live but your inner-universe would not be responding. Luckily, our inner-verse is very responsive to our consciousness and such an event would be very unlikely. That of course, is just it. The cells of our bodies listen well and surrender to our consciousness.

When you look around your life and experience love for those you hold dear, feel compassion for your fellow man, mourn in your heart at the sight of others suffering or give of yourself to help the greater good, which force do you think feels the same for you? It holds such love for you. It would never approach you if it felt you might fear it. It would never reveal itself if it felt you were not seeking it. It would never enter into you if it felt, deep in your heart, it was not invited. If you do not choose the Force, it will respect your decision, even if your choice would cause it harm.

When we read about some of the great enlightened masters of the past, Jesus, Buddha, Krishna, we note similar traits. Compassion, devotion and an overwhelming sense that these people were more than human; these beings were the fingertips of God. In the beginning, were they so very different than we are now? You already know what the difference was.

They made a choice.

They surrendered to that choice absolutely and unconditionally. They chose the Force and raised their consciousness to its tonal. The Force accepted them and worked through them to shape reality and change the course of this world.

When someone looks at the Universe and accepts both the Force and anti-matter they have declared their neutrality. They have, to put it bluntly, spiritually neutered themselves and removed any possibility for the Force to fully move into them and procreate or direct its will through them as a willing vessel.

This serves the purpose of the Darkside well.

Its first option for destroying life is to turn the creation of matter against itself. The second option is to convince as much life as possible to accept destruction as inevitable, to get them to stand on the sidelines of the battle and do nothing.

By accepting a non-dualistic position, we are putting our consciousness in a stasis. We can begin the journey of expanding our consciousness and we may experience deep relaxation or feelings of bliss but we can never enter levels of true enlightenment. When we refuse to embrace the Force this ensures that we will never awaken and serve the purpose of a White Cell.

By choosing to act neither for the Force nor for the Darkside, we cannot experience the many higher vibrations that exist within God and we will have made the success of the Darkside more possible.

Through time, the Darkside has turned many White Cells away from the path of awakening so that they lose their way and cannot fulfill their purpose. It may seem simple, very black and white, but anyone who holds to a non-dualistic belief ensures that awakening is impossible.

THE STRUGGLE OF GOD

The idea of the Force and a counter-force, or reaction of anti-matter can all seem very abstract to some people. Because I want everyone to understand these concepts, let us imagine that you are God, only as a human. You are in a rainforest, teeming with life. You are in this rainforest exploring, examining plants and animals, experiencing all of the wonderful and strange forms of life that are everywhere.

Suddenly your path takes an unfortunate turn; you are up to your chest in quicksand and fighting for your life.

At that moment, what do you think the quicksand would be to you? Would you consider it your friend? Could you consider something like quicksand being capable of being your friend or your enemy? It has no conscious personality, no specific intention driven by an ego. Now ask yourself, even without a conscious intention, does it have a purpose? Its purpose is to do what quicksand does. There is only one possible outcome if we accept being in the quicksand, so it does offer us something.

Death is its only offering. That is the Darkside. The quicksand is the Darkside. The struggling explorer is God.

If you fell into quicksand what do you expect your first thought would be? You must survive. God is no different. Your first reaction is to escape but struggling against quicksand only sucks you in faster. That is life. Life wants to survive but if God acts too quickly, the reaction from the quicksand will destroy it.

Your survival is entirely dependant upon a state of mind.

You have to think of the one thing that will help you to escape. That is what God is trying to do. It is trying to find a way to ensure that it survives. It is desperate to do it. The trick of this situation is you cannot fight quicksand, or the Darkside, in the direct way that you want. However, it can be fought, but in a different way. You have to stop thinking in a conventional way. You have to think outside of the box in a way far different from how you normally think. Because your normal body movement will not help you, it is vital to creatively consider other options. There are things that you can do. Unfortunately, it is rare to find the necessary answers.

When faced with destruction your desire focuses on survival. If you could get out of this quicksand, you would happily continue your journey through the jungle with renewed spirit. There is still so much to experience.

First, you must escape the quicksand, which has no conscious intention but will be your doom all the same. It has a divine purpose as a reaction to your having fallen into it.

God came into this dimension and the reaction to its creation is attempting to smother it back out of existence in this dimension. The quicksand may not know or care that it is trying to kill you, but your reflection does give it life. How you acknowledge it through your reaction is it reflecting your reaction back to you. It is a mirror and it gets its intelligence from you. Suddenly it occurs to you 'This thing is trying to kill me, it has a plan for me!' What is its plan? Death! It seems to outthink your every move! When you push down it sucks you even further, it does not push you up in the way everything else does. It is completely opposite of everything else that you are used to.

Now you are desperate, completely desperate to survive, just as the Universe is.

There is, of course, a way out of quicksand. If you panic, death is certain. You have to be cautious, careful and make slow movements. This is a state of mind more than literal physical movements. Ironically, these methods reflect all of my teachings. It parallels them. The point is that the quicksand is a living thing in one aspect. It probably has living organisms in it. It has a degree of intention. Consider it the most basic kind of intelligence. What is intelligence anyway, but a vast array of reactions and non-reactions based upon actions. So you could look at it and say it is just quicksand but it does have a purpose behind it. That intention is none other than, the intention to simply suck the Universe under and destroy us all.

That is the Darkside and it has intelligence because we give it intelligence. How God must deal with the Darkside helps us understand how we must deal with life to find God. We cannot struggle and fight to fully awaken the way we would expect.

Here, in this analogy, we have become aware of a broader struggle. On a Universal level and on a smaller, more personal level, everything reflects this struggle. We must become aware of these two forces. One, of which we are a part, is struggling to survive and experience. The other is reacting to it and pulling life under.

For those who accept the non-dualistic point of view, seeing neither good nor evil, I pose a question. If you fall into the quicksand, does it matter? I mean, you could just ignore it and it would go away wouldn't it? Is it going to go away? No. Does it still have intention for you? Yes. Could it fool you and tell you, yeah, just relax you are not sinking, but really what are you doing very slowly? You just do not feel it.

You can sit there and think that you and the quicksand are one and you are just balancing each other and refuse to acknowledge this reality if you like. While you do, you are up to your neck choking on quicksand.

We must choose the Force if we are to move through it and it through us.

We must surrender to it and accept we are a part of it. We must be willing to allow it to work with us and then and only then can our consciousness enter the high vibrations of enlightenment. Anyone who holds to these non-dualistic beliefs and believes they have found enlightenment is quite mistaken. They are in a stasis and moving in a circle where they can go no further.

To those people I say, you have not even begun to see the wonder that awaits you, and you have not even begun to feel what it is to truly be in that place.

Do not fall victim to this way of thinking. Choose the Force and it will show the way.

To allow the Force to move through us we must understand how it will work through us. We must strengthen our connection to our Navigator and connect with our dimensional consciousness. That is where we must begin, understanding the nature of the soul, which is the energy body that we will use to tap the Force.

CHAPTER SEVEN

A SOUL WITHIN

A SOUL WITHIN

*You look around in a distant way and then you listen deeply, breathe
deeply, feel deeply.*

Realize that the most important moment for any of us is the present
one. Change is only possible in the present, right now, right here.
This is where you begin. When we try to contemplate the
magnitude of the entire Universe, it is easy to feel small and
possibly lost.

Take heart, you are far greater than you might imagine.

We cannot compare ourselves to this huge cosmic universal
creation spinning off into infinity! Everything can seem so large
and beyond ourselves when we do. It does not matter! What
matters, truly, is what is here now.

We need to understand enough of the levels to know what is

important here and now and to realize anti-matter will ruin this divine plan if it has its way. It does not want us to progress back to energy. It wants us to stop the progression because it is the opposite of all reactions. That is why there is a struggle.

The Force is striving to push life forward in the same way our bodies fight to live. Life is a struggle whether it is our bodies struggling to maintain physical health or it is the Force trying to progress the Universe. At this point you might be feeling powerless. We are so small in comparison to everything, how can we make a difference? It is probably comforting to hear and know that the only things that matter are before us right now, at this moment.

The challenge we face in this moment is to understand the struggle to awaken, to connect with the elements that will begin to satisfy our spiritual needs.

A sense of purpose drives the need that will lead us to connect with our dimensional consciousness. The Universe instills in you a sense of purpose because it is of great importance that you awaken.

Always remember, do not discount a thing because of its perceived size. At this moment, you may view yourself as a relatively small thing, but you hold near limitless potential.

To awaken we must understand what we are as spiritual beings, how we evolve, and grow.

WHAT IS A SPIRITUAL BEING?

To begin to understand what we are as spiritual beings, let us re-examine our physical beings. As we have discussed, the human body is a robot of sorts with the energy being controlling it. Try not to let your relationship to your body get in the way of seeing the truth of this.

While our design is soft, organic flesh, the process involved in working the body is similar to how we control other tools we have made. From the time we are born into this world, we spend great amounts of time and energy training our bodies to respond to our will. After a time, the body responds almost perfectly as we desire it to. This is why the idea that the center of our being resides within a dimensional consciousness that exists apart from our body is often such a challenging concept.

This idea is so challenging it requires us to put forth effort to truly understand that we are energy beings. As energy beings, we experience the physical world as energy that the body translates. The energy being registers physical sensations and experiences as electrical signals received from nerves. Without the body, an energy being would be very limited in its ability to experience and grow.

An energy being cannot make noise, at least not as we know it, because as energy it does not have vocal cords. Nor would it have lungs to propel sound, or eyes to see as we see, or eardrums to hear as we do. To explore this dimension we connected our energy bodies to our current bodies. The brain became the driver's seat, much like the one we would sit in to control a car. Once we have a physical body, as energy beings, we can explore and experience this dimension in ways not otherwise possible.

Your hands and other parts of your body collect data, translate these experiences into energy, and send it along to your brain. Once the brain receives this energy, it translates the data, which creates the experience. This process is necessary for your energy being to be able to experience this dimension. In fact, because science can observe this whole process of converting experiences into electricity or energy you should find it easier to acknowledge and realize the truth of what you are.

Your being is conscious, living energy.

Physical evidence of the energy body exists and a number of different sources document it. The first of these is Russian engineer Semyan Kirlian who discovered that living tissue emits electromagnetic force fields that show up on photosensitive paper. The process of photographing and recording this is called Kirlian photography.

Using his photographic technique, a leaf with a portion of it cut out still shows the outline of its missing part. Even though it is not there, physically, the photograph shows an outline as if it was.

This prompts suggestions that Kirlian photography reveals the energy body.

Kirlian photographs show energy emanating from the body. A picture of a hand, for example, depicts the fingers illuminated by energy. If two people touch fingertips, the energy appears to fight until both people accept the presence of the other.

Another interesting case involves people who have amputated feet and legs. These people frequently report intense pain originating from phantom limbs. When a person places their hand on the area of pain, where the missing limb would be, and massages it as if there was a hand or limb there the pain stops.

At the point of death the human body inexplicably loses several ounces of weight. Studies have also shown that when photographed with light sensitive film, for an amount of nanoseconds, less than a second, a large illumination expands from the body and disappears upon death.

These examples all point toward the conclusion that a separate body or being composed of energy inhabits the physical human body.

Why energy? Energy is one property that is common to all life. Much of the energy on Earth comes from the sun in the form of light. This light travels from the sun through space as photons and collides with the Earth. Plants convert photons into energy through photosynthesis. This energy becomes fruits, edible grains, leaves, or other forms of plant life.

At the heart of all of this life is energy.

The key to the true nature of a spiritual being is not in energy alone, as that exists in all life universally. The key is in the transformation of it. Energy, according to physics, cannot be destroyed, only changed into different forms. Life on Earth, in its many forms, contains energy from the sun. Energy animates all human life and some consider this energy a soul. Really it is just an electrical body of sorts, for everyone to experience life.

Now, if a soul is energy, and an electrical body is energy, then what is the difference? What creates the distinction that marks a white cell and a spiritual being? We live, love, cry, dream, desire and go through all of the wonderful things that life has to offer. However, these shared experiences are not enough to create a dimensional consciousness or soul.

The difference between a soul and an electrical energy body, which everyone has, is that the soul is a developed dimensional body.

The soul is manifesting, or vibrating, at a higher frequency than our physical bodies and thoughts. All energy separates into different patterns, rhythms, and frequencies. Because the soul is energy, it can change its pattern or frequency through refinement.

It can be developed and transformed. Are you beginning to see the larger picture and true nature of what a spiritual being is?

A spiritual being is a developed consciousness of pure, eternal energy exploring this dimension of physical matter.

EVOLUTION OF A SOUL

The essence of our being, our soul, is purely energy and when the body dies it is the soul that can carry on our existence. For how long this might be possible is unknowable, but scientists have speculated about the possibility of maintaining consciousness in the form of energy after the body has died. If our soul holds together after death, we can join with a new body and remain in this dimension.

Reincarnation is the process of having our soul move from one life and becoming reborn into another after death. I believe that upon death we do not have to immediately reincarnate. If we are strong enough, we can exist for any amount of time outside of the body as a being of pure energy. The essential element of this process is that we must have a highly developed energy body.

Why should a soul go through this process rather than just experience it as a pure energy being?

Our souls are trying to evolve and move to a higher consciousness. To do this we need to collect data. Our soul takes information, smells, sights, and sounds, everything it cannot get as energy, and learns from it. The soul grows in this way, by taking data from the body, life after life.

One of the most powerful ways to experience is through emotion. Emotion is largely biochemical reactions created by the body. As energy beings, we would completely miss the things we hold so dear: love, passion, or hope. Even things like fear can be wonderful to feel, it helps us to know courage! As energy beings, we would never know emotion, the way we experience it now. Each life presents the soul with new experiences.

This is how the soul hopes to advance its consciousness, by evolving life after life to arrive at a more perfect understanding of reality.

To really understand where the soul hopes to ultimately go, first we will look at where the soul has come from. The universe is the body of God and we know that we exist within that body. God experiences through this dimension and its awareness moves throughout it. Now relate this to our bodies. Every electron returns collected data to our brain, which adds to our collective consciousness. Our soul performs a similar function for the collective consciousness of God.

Our journeys through this dimension, in the form of many lifetimes, collect experiences, which eventually return to the consciousness of God.

As we experience we begin to vibrate, which is the frequency of our energy body, at a frequency that is closer to the vibration of God. We become the imagination of God, much like the electrons of the brain, collecting data from a remote part of our physical body then adding to our consciousness by reporting its data. This data is collected, interpreted and eventually becomes an experience. We are the electrons to God. The reality of this process is much more complicated than this explanation but in some ways as simple.

All souls have come from the creation of God or the creation of the Universe.

This includes anything that has a soul, from life scattered throughout the entire universe, and is not limited to human beings. Life on Earth began from sunlight, from the photosynthesis of energy. Plants and trees gathered energy and transferred it to other life as they consumed them. This includes human beings, which became a part of the biological life of the planet.

Our thoughts and emotions were like that of a dog or cat. They consisted of biochemical reactions in the brain of varying complexities. These reactions gave us feelings and emotions that we mimicked from others when we were young.

We developed and formed social relationships with others but this does not mean we had a soul. We had energy that moved through our bodies that performed all of the things required for survival but that energy was not developed.

Then one day we began to ponder this energy, and formed the concept of a soul. We started to experience and understand ourselves as something other than a creature completely concerned with existing. As we reflected on our inner-dimension, the idea of what a soul really was began to emerge. If, in this life, we attain awareness, if we understand life from a higher perspective, and realize our nature as an energy being then we have begun the creation of a soul.

When we die this energy, because we have inwardly reflected upon it, lets us exist outside of our body.

Thinking about our energy being is like building a muscle. Thought and reflection exercises it, flexes it and makes it grow stronger. Once detached from the physical body, which is truly possible only at death, the energy being instinctually searches for another vessel. The energy being reacts to death with an instinct to continue its existence.

It will seek out another body as quickly as possible because, as anything in life, it wants to live.

Before we die we must learn all we can, to maintain our soul. Simply knowing what a soul is does not mean you will know how to control it. Information alone is not enough.

How long did it take you to learn how to walk? Have you ever seen an adult show a baby how they walk and then watch as the baby tries to mimic it? How often do you see the baby slap itself on the forehead after the adult gives them the example, exclaiming, 'Oh, I get it! How simple.' and then proceeds to run quickly after the adult? You never see that because it is not that easy.

Do you think maintaining and controlling your soul is any different?

Think about how long it takes someone to learn how to drive a car. Do you see people just jump in a car, turn the key and zip off down the road obeying all traffic laws their very first time? No. It takes time and effort to learn how to drive and likewise developing a soul takes time and dedication.

If we have put effort, thought and energy into developing our spiritual self for thirty years before we die then certainly, we should not have any reason to be concerned about the survival of our soul. However, if we began to realize and reflect on our spiritual nature later in life we need to put forth extra energy and effort in order to have enough time for our energy to function outside of the body.

Thinking about our soul creates it, inside of us, as a secondary life.

The essence of our being is energy, our bodies are equipped to manipulate and control energy. The design of our bodies allows them to contain energy, by reflecting on and being aware of energy in the world around us, we are consuming energy. Once our body consumes and stores the energy, it then controls it to do what it wants.

Imagine if we had to consciously manipulate the energy in our bodies to perform all of the functions that it executes without our direct interaction or knowledge. This would be an extremely difficult task! Our design is phenomenal in its automation!

Now think about if we did start to exercise control over our energy. If we can control this energy without thinking about it, we can certainly start taking our mind, which is energy, and design a structure of energy and train it to exist beyond the physical body.

The ultimate goal of training our soul to exist after our body dies is to continue our existence beyond the death of our physical body. We do not have to accept the idea that everyone has one life to experience. We estimate the universe to be about fifteen billion years old. The average life expectancy of a human being is about sixty-five to eighty-six years old. If we compare the scale of these time spans we should quickly conclude that there is simply no way that anyone can expect to experience the full spectrum of possibilities in just one life. We might as well say that a newborn baby has experienced all life has to offer in its first thirty minutes of life!

The truth of our existence is far more comforting and beautiful. There is a progression and evolution of our soul if we choose to reflect upon it and engage in that process.

YOU DECIDE THE DESTINY OF YOUR SOUL

When we die, we recollect the totality of our true self, so we become aware of all of our past lives. This in return expands our consciousness. We do not become someone different. The identity we have at this very moment, the person reading this book merges into one consciousness after we die. Our current identity merges into the totality of all that we truly are.

It is like reading a novel.

We go along with the main character of the book sharing in all of their adventures and experiences. Once we finish the book, in some aspects, we are the same. In other ways we have changed, perhaps the book inspires us to have a different outlook on life. We have certainly changed by adding their experiences to our own. Who we are is intact. We are a contributor to the whole picture as much as a blood cell is individual and yet part of the whole of our body.

By progressing from life to life we can gain a much greater variety of experiences than if we lived a single life forever. Imagine the impact of living one life as a man and the next as a woman. That one change would create an incredibly different experience. It gives you an experience that you could never have had in a single life, even if you lived for hundreds of years.

Consider how large the world is and how many different people are living a life dramatically different from your own. There is no substitute for experience and each life offers much that you will never truly know, or feel, unless you live it.

Only by making a conscious effort can we develop our souls so that they might continue forward upon the death of our physical bodies.

Unfortunately, we are often afraid to fully accept this because we fear the responsibility and the power placed in our hands. We control the destiny of our soul. We decide if we will move on after our bodies' death.

Society conditions us through television, movies, and various belief systems to accept that we cannot decide our destiny. Often this takes the form of a belief that some higher power decides who goes on and who does not or that we are immortal from the moment we are born. These beliefs will prevent us from moving forward if we accept their limitations. Some people simply choose to never consider the inevitability of their death. For the soul to evolve we must achieve a state of openness so that we can really work on ourselves.

It may be hard to imagine bridging over from a physical body to an energy body.

Although it might seem like a big jump, the physical reality is that we have already died. Depending on how old you are physically, you may have died multiple times. You are not the same body that you were before. In fact, the person you used to be does not even exist. According to science your body, cell for cell, has died and been replaced about every 5 years, give or take a few years. Every cell in your brain, everything in your eye, everything is replaced every five years.

We might not see it all at once but one day we will look in the mirror and say, 'I don't look anything like I used to'. Look at an old picture! All of us go from being very small baby structures to this big gigantic adult body and our mass and structure of energy changes dramatically. We want the energy body to continue to change, even after death we want it to evolve instead of collapsing. If we cannot envision our physical body bridging over into a body of energy, we will not evolve. Is your physical body so very important that you cannot imagine abandoning it?

It is a fear of letting go that holds you here. It is petty to allow that one simple fear to halt the evolution of a soul, but it will.

Reflect on how the energy being functions and dedicate effort to become more. We are energy beings. By believing in spirituality, we allow ourselves to feel spiritual. When you feel spiritual, your consciousness moves at a higher frequency. That is why you feel different when you are being spiritual. Most people are simply not aware of exactly why they feel different. It is the vibration of our consciousness shifting.

Belief will raise our tonal and will make us more aware of and open to the possibilities of our being. As our tonal rises, we are able to perceive more, which confirms our belief, which secures our tonal speed and maintains it. It is a self-feeding process but to initiate this process we must first believe, or at least be open to the possibility, and be aware.

Without an open mind our energy or tonal moves at a lower vibration because how, and what, we think affects the tonal of our consciousness. At a lower tonal we are oblivious to the higher dimensions. We cannot see or feel the things that we could, were our tonal not standing still.

Belief in our spiritual nature is the essential step to beginning this process of increasing our tonal but let me be clear about what I mean by 'belief'. I do not mean to instantly or blindly believe in spirituality or any other concept discussed in this book. I would never suggest that a person must have faith in any of these concepts simply because I say they are so. Do not accept blind faith; I never have. I have always questioned everything and strongly encourage you to do the same. This is why I feel so strongly in delivering a solid, logical explanation of how the Universe works and giving others the tools to have their own experiences.

When a person has experiences, it will be up to them to interpret those experiences on the intellectual grounding of this book or some other foundation. In the end, I have little doubt their experiences will validate that what I am saying is true.

True faith is acquired through experience and understanding.

A person might not believe in entities and that is fine, but does that person allow for the possibility that an entity might exist? We can look at it like an elementary school science project. Our hypothesis is that a being made purely of some form of energy, but self-aware and conscious, could exist. Then we begin to test that hypothesis, first by examining possible ways an entity might work, exist and experience.

At this point in the process, belief is optional.

Once I reveal ways to encounter or experience entities, the next step will be to follow through with those steps and make an open-minded effort to encounter one face to face. Nobody else would even need to be around. Now if you sat, face-to-face, with an entity could you then say that they existed? When a person encounters an entity directly like this, if they are open to believe they should be able to acknowledge that they exist.

This experience might leave a person with more questions about how or what their experience was but most could feel confident and begin to build faith based on this experience.

Because people, in general, are so educated now the intellect makes the consciousness more grounded. This can work against us as we attempt to explore things that many consider irrational because we are telling our brains to tune out frequencies of reality that we do not believe are possible. Our brains obediently block out these other dimensions or frequencies of energy.

By being open enough to accept the possibility of the Force, by trying to experience it, by trying to sense it, by trying to feel the Force, we open ourselves to a higher vibration, which means that we will experience more.

This is why an atheist or someone who does not allow the belief of certain things is likely to never experience something paranormal or dimensional, where as a non-atheist or spiritual person could. It is because a person's energy, at a different frequency, directly affects what their awareness allows. By believing and accepting the possibility of other dimensions, we can see dimensions more easily than a person who does not accept the possibility can. It does not mean we have to believe to begin our exploration, but the more we can chip away at our non-belief by having experiences, the more it opens us up to many other things because we can tune into a greater range of frequencies of energy.

THE GOVERNOR

Now, clever people will probably try to tell themselves that they can force themselves to believe. It is not that easy. If we could force ourselves to believe, there would be no reason for the Navigator. Inside we will always doubt things.

The 'governor' is something inside our brain, which resists our attempts to change our fundamental ideas about reality.

It is like a control mechanism or filter. It holds us here, at this dimensional frequency. There have been devices placed within cars called governors that limit the car's maximum speed. We have a similar mechanism in our brains. Our bodies and brains are products of this dimension, this frequency, and are wired to perceive and interact only in this dimension. The governor acts to limit our experience to this frequency and filter out all other dimensions from our awareness.

Think of when we talked about cars on a freeway to understand dimensions. The governor is set to limit the speed of your vehicle. It wants to keep you at the speed of this dimension, which could be 10 M.P.H. Meanwhile, all of these cars or other dimensions are zipping by you at 20, 50, 100 M.P.H and you will never be aware of what is going on inside of them. An entity can be in the same room that we are, but because it is vibrating at a higher tonal, our governor will block it from our senses.

As we begin to understand and realize the truth of the governor, we can train our awareness to allow us to perceive different frequencies.

When we accept new concepts about the nature of reality, it changes the governor so that it begins to let us experience new frequencies. There are also many techniques and ways of slipping past or fooling the governor. These are back doors, which are useful in allowing us to experience things before we have fully realized them. There are too many ways and the details are too long for this book to cover. For now, it is important to simply note that such possibilities exist. Many ritual-based philosophies, like Magick, work on this principle. The governor is powerful because it is a part of our brain and is the very thing that controls how we think!

To directly confront it is foolish.

We can stare at a wall for days and try to convince ourselves it is not solid or that our body is not all that we are and we will still never truly believe it. The first step in breaking the governor down is to acknowledge that it exists. By doing this, we identify the governor and our mind is more able to slip past it.

Here is a simple brainteaser, which may help illustrate the power of the governor. Read the sentence below and count aloud the F's in the sentence. Count them only once. Do not go back and count them again.

SCIENTIFIC FORMULAS OF ANY KIND FREQUENTYLY TAKE YEARS OF RESEARCH TO DEFINE AFTER STUDYING THE RESULTS OF MANY TESTS.

Do you think you know how many F's there were? I will tell you in a moment. Much of our thinking runs on automatic as our brain does its own processing. There was a study done on a man who, because of a car crash, had impaired vision on the right side even though both of his eyes were perfectly fine. He could not see anything out of his right eye. After much testing, doctors found that his brain was receiving signals and was aware of everything occurring on his right side, as if he could see. Somehow, he was not consciously aware of it.

What are we unaware of that the brain perceives?

Can we control, or remove, the governor from filtering of our experiences? Yes, we can. By the way, there are eight F's in the above sentence. Many people overlook the "F" in "of" because it sounds like a "V" so that is what the brain delivers.

Reprogramming the governor can be a slow process and the brain resists change more as we grow older. The chances of reaching a dimensional state of mind are against us. How could reaching dimensional states not be extremely difficult? Our bodies, the very vessels we use to experience with, are products and creations of this dimension. This is especially true for highly educated people, who are common in our information driven society. The challenge with education is that the more a person sets boundaries for what they believe to be true, the more rigid that person becomes in their way of thinking.

When a person accumulates large amounts of knowledge they become fixed in their thinking. Changing a person's belief toward something that appears to them to be irrational is a difficult thing to do. People often look for shortcuts to ease the process of altering the governor to achieve a dimensional state. There might be tools and maybe a few tricks to make this process a little easier, but in the end there are no shortcuts.

Unfortunately, some supposed 'shortcuts' also carry great risks for the mind and body of the person who chooses to follow them. Specifically, I am talking about the use of consciousness altering drugs or psychedelics. These drugs draw people who have a spiritual nature because the experience that they provide can feel dimensional and therefore familiar. These experiences can give them a glimpse past their governor but there is a great danger in using any type of drug. Drugs often derail the seeker and permanently crystallize their consciousness. All that they offer are mimicked glimpses of what some spiritual experiences are like. By choosing the easy route, a person ensures that they will reap the results of that easy effort.

Fast food spirituality delivers junk enlightenment that leads nowhere.

Nothing can do it for you. Not technology, not drugs. It is the lazy route and it is a dead end. By understanding spirits, entities, energy, and the paranormal and by taking these concepts in small stages we can begin to feel more of the Force. This becomes the catalyst of something more intense as we progress spiritually in time. By using drugs, even if we see things, it does not mean that we will fully digest and understand them.

When the drugs wear off our governor is still there, active and able as ever.

True awakening or dimensional consciousness cannot be an instantaneous event. If we are not prepared for an experience, the governor will find a way to explain, dismiss or block it out. It is up to the individual to personally take the steps required to achieve a permanent understanding. Anything you use that artificially alters your consciousness without firm grounded understanding of how consciousness works or how the whole universe breaks down will always fail in the end. They will never be able to fully awaken you.

You will become dependent on using the drug or technological device as a tool to regain or maintain the state of consciousness it allows you to experience. In other words, the tool opens a door in your consciousness and you go in that door and experience what lies beyond it. However, because you lack the universal truth and experience to understand how the door was opened or what it really is, the tool you used has become your key and only way back in. That key only opens one door, no matter how differently the experience manifests itself.

A true spiritual experience begins to show you the nature of all the many doors of the mind and flowers beyond that one experience. It takes energy and effort to manipulate a person's governor so that they can have true spiritual experiences on their own. To progress on a spiritual level realize that we are spiritual beings and then decide how far along the path you wish to go.

To reach enlightenment we must bridge the familiar physical dimension with the higher dimensions that we are striving to understand. This process requires time. It could take weeks, months, years, or even lifetimes. We must reflect on this knowledge until our soul is developed and our mind is ready to become a higher frequency.

If we damage our brain or body with drugs or other activities, we become severely limited.

The brain is the bridge to our soul or dimensional consciousness. If a car that we are driving becomes damaged it can still be driven, but will have flaws in its performance and capability. We may try to fix it but the damage may be beyond repair. Our bodies are like cars for the soul, and if they are injured, we may not be able to recover from the damage that they have sustained. We can continue to drive a damaged car but our journeys may be limited. We cannot damage the soul inhabiting our bodies but we can injure the tools that our bodies provide to explore this world. It is unfortunate but we all must continue, so take care of your vessel.

For the sake of simplicity, I have referred to our energy being as a single thing, made up of a single energy body. I have called it our soul or dimensional consciousness. In truth, we have many energy bodies. The process of developing these energy bodies will ultimately lead us to reconnect with the dimensional, and finally, hyper-dimensional consciousness.

Remember that our consciousness is energy moving in varying frequencies, as our soul evolves it will vibrate at higher and higher frequencies and will become closer to the vibration of the Force.

When we awaken, part of what happens is that our current consciousness begins to merge with our dimensional consciousness. This is our reemergence into the collective and totality of who we truly are.

When we begin to remember all that we have forgotten, all that our pure energy consciousness knows we will have begun to awaken.

But, why must we go through the process of awakening at all? Why are we not born with the recollection of all of our past lives? Why is there a disconnection between our conscious mind and our dimensional consciousness? If we urgently need white cells to ensure the survival of life, why are they not born with all they need to know?

Many questions remain about the process of awakening and the nature of White Cells. Now that we have discussed what a soul is, how a soul can evolve and develop and how it can exist outside of the physical body, we can begin to discuss the 'Sleeper'.

CHAPTER EIGHT

MIGRATION OF THE SLEEPER

MIGRATION OF THE SLEEPER

It is then that you know there is a veil between you and some other place that holds an understanding to that which you are.

As a Sleeper, you can awaken and connect to your dimensional consciousness, but you have yet to fully realize this potential. You are in a sleep, a sleep that is far from ordinary. What you do not know yet is why. Now you know that some part of your being, the Navigator, exists to help rouse you from that sleep. The Navigator guides you toward experiences and knowledge that will aid in your awakening.

As our journey returns to the point at which we started, we must look more closely at the Sleeper. A Sleeper is someone who has a Navigator but has not yet realized what they truly are. It is someone who has not yet chosen to accept their higher purpose. It is one who does not understand the reason they are asleep.

It is time to understand.

During the course of our time together, I have revealed many amazing things! We exist within a being, Gaia, and the body of God, which is the universe. The greater being of God is a multi-dimensional state filled with universes, and this universe is only a part of that being. The reaction to the creation of God in this dimension is the Darkside, which opposes all life. Finally, we have discussed the nature of our soul and dimensional consciousness.

Reading about these things exhilarates a Sleeper! It is as if they have spent their whole life searching for something. Never quite able to put their finger on what it is, they know that life, somehow, does not feel complete. It is as if there should be more, dimensionally or physically, something beyond it all.

When we start to find pieces of this puzzle, it feeds our dimensional consciousness and the Navigator tells us, 'Yes, now I remember, this is the way.' The more lives we have lived, the more aware our dimensional consciousness is and the more influence it can exert in this life to guide us. The older souls, those who have lived many lives, carry knowledge from existing as dimensional beings, some of them on other worlds. They are like light Sleepers and are restless to 'wake up'. These older beings often display more awareness and pursue their spirituality from a very young age.

The Sleeper is the part of our being that we so often search and yearn for but easily forget.

THE SECRET KEY

We cannot see the sleeper with our eyes, regardless of how hard we try. We cannot feel it with our hands, hear it with our ears, or directly experience it with any of our five senses. We could travel the world over and still never find it. Many have tried.

The Sleeper is within you.

It does not exist within your body. It exists within your being. It exists in a place your five senses cannot take you. It is dimensional. The Universe actually needs you to forget and fall into this state of sleep, which I will explain in a moment. However, the Universe also needs a way for you to reconnect with and awaken the Sleeper.

It left you a secret key.

Do you want to know what this key is? What if I told you it is something you already have? In fact, it is something you have probably heard of before but cast it aside. Perhaps others discouraged you from using it. I wonder what you will do with it if I tell you. Will you listen to your Navigator and use it or push it back under the doormat and forever lock yourself out from awakening? The Universe gave us all a sense so that we can move to the place where the Sleeper exists and bring back the knowledge we needed. It gave us the sixth sense. The sixth sense is the missing link that will open the door to awakening.

We are all psychic. I do not mean to say we all can read minds or bend spoons with our will. I mean to say that we all have the potential to harness profound levels of sensory. We can shift our consciousness into other states by using the sixth sense and exercising our paranormal abilities.

Instead of pursuing this potential, many choose to sleep. We live in a dream. We do not remember who we really are. Our dimensional consciousness is who we really are and it is waiting for us to connect with it and awaken. How do we connect with our dimensional consciousness? How does a Sleeper awaken?

The Navigator tells us what we need to do.

It guides and directs us through life, and we must learn to enhance that sense. We must enhance the sixth sense. Every enlightened master or awakened being has displayed some level of paranormal ability! Think about how many accounts there are of great teachers or masters, performing amazing miraculous feats! Is it a coincidence that all of these beings had profound paranormal abilities?

These masters made their discoveries because they understood and made use of their sixth sense.

Rediscovering and learning how to use our psychic abilities is the final step in awakening. These abilities are the tools we use to bridge our brains with our minds, and awaken dimensional consciousness.

FORGOTTEN BRIDGE: THE SIXTH SENSE LEADS TO AWAKENING

Many eastern philosophies, and western for that matter, believe the pursuit of paranormal powers is a waste of time. They think that psychic abilities are meaningless or, in some cases, a negative ego-filled pursuit. Others have gone so far as to say that experiencing paranormal events is a dead-end that holds no merit. When I hear such nonsense, I almost need to hit myself in the head with a board just to make sure I really heard correctly! How can anyone, seriously pursuing that state of enlightenment, suggest such a thing?

Every account of a truly enlightened teacher, ties their awakening with the manifestation of paranormal effects.

It is beyond absurd to even consider that such abilities are meaningless! There are stories about these beings walking on water, healing the sick, seeing the future, levitating, journeying to worlds of light and many other such descriptions, the list is long. Yet, many schools of thought still brush paranormal abilities aside as a waste of time or something that distracts a Sleeper from awakening.

Awakening to a higher state of consciousness directly relates to the emergence of paranormal abilities.

I started to think about why there is such a strong negative fixation on this matter and came to some interesting conclusions. Consider the general intelligence, concerns, and fears of an average person in ancient times. The Mystery schools, holy shrines, or temples were as financially dependant on the general populace then as they are now. If they were not dependant directly on the people, they were dependent on the rulers of the time. Because they were dependent on people, they were also sensitive to the concerns and fears of those people. People often fear things that they do not understand.

When people were creating these theologies, they did not understand paranormal abilities. The reason that these ridiculous beliefs about paranormal abilities exist today is that people still do not understand what paranormal abilities are, how natural they are, and for that reason, people are still afraid. I can imagine the mobs with torches surrounding the temples now!

The mystical masters knew this and understood that the common man did not have the intellect to comprehend what they were experiencing and seeking. They knew that appearances were everything and they needed a good public image. This was especially true if they wanted funding without crowds of fearful people, with aggressive ideas, at their doorstep. They created an image and doctrine they felt the general populace could accept.

Then they created levels within the organization and kept some of those levels secret from the public.

Every spiritual organization has secret teachings or doctrines. These very secret doctrines often hold the keys to the pursuit of paranormal experiences and abilities!

The point is; it was necessary to publicly deny and discourage the pursuit of paranormal abilities because it might have created hysteria in the people who supported the religious centers. These organizations initiated and slowly exposed new members to these hidden paranormal teachings based on intellect and level of trust. For thousands of years this system has been supported and the message against the pursuit of paranormal abilities has been refined during that time.

Today we consider it common sense that a person should not pursue metaphysical abilities!

At a time when fear and mass hysteria were common it was understandable to use secrecy as a defense against persecution. Why nobody has stepped up to the plate to sort this all out in the modern era is a puzzle to me. This secrecy is still in place and it is a cause for the failure in achieving spiritual enlightenment!

To awaken we must use the sixth sense, to interpret and unfold our awakening just as we use the five senses.

Our sixth sense is missing, lost through evolution. We have five senses that interpret sound, taste, touch, smell and sight but without the sixth sense that interprets the paranormal, we lack the ability to be complete. Spiritual seekers often sit and meditate on nothing, hoping that at some random moment, they will suddenly awaken. A seeker is not actively pursuing awakening by taking this path, with no direction. They are attempting to stumble upon the path of enlightenment by shedding the five senses.

Consider this, if by chance a person does experience an awakening by this method, will it not be a paranormal event when it happens? What is more, if that moment arrives, what sense will they use to experience and interpret the data they are receiving? If your consciousness shifts closer to the tonal of the Force, which is energy, will you be able to touch it, smell it, taste it, see it or hear it? No. Only your sixth sense will be able to convey the experience.

The seeker must shed the five familiar senses leaving only the sixth sense as a guide.

In the end, the sixth sense delivers awakening and completes us. The five familiar senses receive and deliver data from our immediate dimension. How are these five senses, which are designed to interpret this dimension, going to help once we remove ourselves from our physical body? We need that last sense which works more as a sensory of frequency and vibration to take the experiences we gain from these dimensional moments and bring them down into our physical body. The function of the sixth sense is to interpret other dimensions.

It allows us to experience other dimensions, just as the other senses allow us to experience this dimension.

You should stop and think about what I just said for a moment. This concept is so important that I am going to repeat it for you. The sixth sense allows us to experience other dimensions in the same way that our current senses allow us to experience this one. If it has not hit you yet, let us consider something for a moment. How different do you think you would view life or this reality if you could not touch?

Imagine living your life able to see and hear objects around you, but lack the ability to touch them. You could not feel the wind on your face, the caress of a loved one, this book in your hand or even the chair you are sitting on! Would it be incredible if all of a sudden you could start feeling, after a lifetime of going without?

That is what it is like to use the sixth sense.

Meditation, knowledge, and mantras all fail in the end without an active sixth sense. The bridge that connects our mind to our hyper-dimensional consciousness is the sixth sense.

FROM OUR PRIMAL PAST TO A DORMANT POTENTIAL

Time has worked against us. In our early stages, humanity was nomadic. We did not communicate in the kind of language that we use now. Instead, early humans would have used various grunts and body motions to communicate.

We were more sensitive to our psychic ability at this time because we relied on it for survival. We certainly were not at the top of the food chain. We did not have claws, as other animals did, or sharp teeth, or speed, or much at all. As an animal, we did not have very much going for us. Our keen psychic awareness was the best defense against animals that were capable of attacking and killing us.

If not for this psychic sense, the human race would not be here today.

It was this constant state of fear that pushed our awareness forward. It was essential for survival. Our primal animal instincts arose from our sixth sense. As human beings have become increasingly dependent on technology for survival and comfort, the sixth sense has become less vital.

Now, if we want food, we do not have to track down our prey through the wilderness. If we want water there is no scouring for a source fearing we will die of thirst, we just turn on the faucet. When you walk outside your home to do a simple chore, like fetch the mail, are you constantly looking around, fearing a giant lion will leap out of the bushes and eat you? No. Humans are at the top of the food chain. We fill our lives with comforts never dreamt of by our primitive ancestors. That is what separates us from the sixth sense. We have lost it; it has become dormant, from lack of use.

We retain the potential to reactivate it.

As human beings evolved, we began to develop the frontal lobe, a part of the brain behind the forehead. What the frontal lobe did was give us creative imagination. The frontal lobe separated us from the animal kingdom and made it possible to invent complicated tools, weapons and traps. We created more tools for safety using the frontal lobe and became less dependent on our instincts or natural psychic ability.

This loss was complete when spiritual doctrines hid the pursuit of paranormal abilities, which relied on the sixth sense, from the public. To this day, a Sleeper must shave away the decay of old ways to breathe again. We must activate our sixth sense to rouse the Sleeper, to awaken!

By combining the frontal lobe with natural instinct, the sixth sense, we can achieve wondrous things, merging the unknown with experience and imagination. Is it not ironic that in the beginning, our ancestors lacked the knowledge to understand it and now we have become too complicated to grasp it? Each of us, you, me, everyone, has an instinct similar to that of our ancestors, which tells us we are more than flesh and blood.

Instinctually we believe in the soul, but the ability to reach it has been lost.

Time, technology, and ignorance have robbed us of it. A true modern-day psychic accomplishes feats by combining animal instinct with the frontal lobe. Like any other talent, some people are born with a more active instinct than others. We could give a group of children an instrument to play and most of them will play horribly. One child might pick it up and play as if they had been practicing for years. Some people are more naturally inclined to be psychically active.

Just as anyone can learn to play an instrument, anyone can learn how to activate and use the sixth sense. If you feel it, if you sense the potential, you have only yourself to blame if you choose to remain ignorant and not pursue the development of this lost sensory. The key is still dormant in you, waiting to re-emerge.

If you wait for society and science to validate the existence of the sixth sense, you will never awaken.

Many people struggle with the idea that they could have any psychic potential because they have never displayed any unusual gift or ability. Most people have never met anyone that ever displayed any kind of psychic or paranormal ability. Who would not doubt the existence of such a thing given the same circumstances! Yet if reflected on, many people find that they believe despite the absence of examples in this world. The Navigator tells us such a thing is possible, it is just a matter of learning how to activate it.

It is our choice, there is no God that chooses who is to be psychic and who is not.

Like all creatures on the Earth, we have a higher sense. When we observe animals we know they are utilizing a sensory humans are not.   Birds follow magnetic fields.   How many humans can instinctually follow magnetic fields?   Dogs have an uncanny ability to sense earthquakes before our best technology. In 1975, the city of Haicheng in China ordered the evacuation of 90,000 city residents because unusual dog behavior alarmed them. Hours later a massive earthquake leveled the city.   An earthquake that measured 7.3 on the Richter scale destroyed around 90 percent of the city's buildings.   Other studies have involved video surveillance of animals anticipating the arrival of their owners regardless of the time of day and without any physical signals. Studies of Canadian wolf packs show that they will attack and kill a wolf in their pack if they sense genetic differences. The list goes on.   Whales, dolphins, apes and all the creatures of this earth innately have this psychic sense.

We are no different.

Beyond the pursuit of spiritual awakening, think about what an enormous impact the sixth sense would have on our daily lives or in society as a whole. The sixth sense would alert us to a loved one in trouble, regardless of distance.   There have been many accounts where mothers will wake up in the middle of the night and feel there is something wrong with their child. They brush it off only to hear later that their child was in a traumatic event like a car wreck.

For business decisions someone could use their heightened sensory to tell if a deal was suspicious or if everyone was being honest.

The sixth sense would clue you in to any kind of trouble.

Even choosing a mate would become easier because you could feel so much more about what that person is really like. The common decision of knowing who to walk up to and even ask out on a date would change as you would sense much more about that person without even speaking to them! This is how early man communicated to begin with and it is an ability we can easily re-tap into now.

If social use of the sixth sense became commonplace our whole world would shift dramatically.

The level of deception and taking advantage of others would vanish as people became better able to read intentions with crystal clarity. Think about the simple task of going to a used car salesman. You could use the sixth sense to tell if they were being deceitful or not! However, if the car salesman also used the sixth sense you could also empathize with their need to make a living and a fair deal would be a certainty.

How we relate as individuals and as nations would be vastly different. Compassion and understanding would rule because our feelings, thoughts and intentions would be open for the world to know. There would be no faking it as the sixth sense reaches internally to the true nature of a person. Our ability to work together as a unified species would be truly inspiring without the levels of fear and mistrust we fight with now.

Life took a very interesting turn when our species lost the connection to the sixth sense. Had we remained connected, the quality of our world would be very different indeed. The rate of this planet's evolution decreased rapidly when we lost our sense that connected us to everything. Consider how different things would be even if women ruled the world rather than men. Women, in general, display much higher levels of intuition and psychic ability. As a result, those with higher levels of intuition are more gentle, understanding and compassionate. Our world would be much more peaceful had they taken leadership. We can only work with the information we have available. This is why men only tend to deal with the world of the five senses and lack the ability to feel the connectivity a woman does. In the end, there is no sense in pointless regret, we must not dwell on where our society could or would have been.

Those of us who feel the urge must begin our own completion.

As people pursue spiritual awakening they also contribute to the whole and the greater good. The Force pushes for the world to reach higher states of consciousness but it will not happen overnight. We must first work on ourselves to reactivate this lost sensory. Activating the sixth sense within your brain and learning how to unite its abilities with the mind will allow you to experience the universe in its full potential. You must not overlook the sixth sense any longer. Its scope reaches far beyond paranormal abilities or spiritual awakening into every aspect and experience of life. It connects them all.

I can explain and teach psychic abilities but you must also seek this knowledge to understand it.

Remember all of the incredible leaps and bounds that humanity has made. As a race, we are still adolescents. What do we really know? Less than 90 years ago, we were using horses and buggies. Reflect back on this and thousands of other oddities in our history. Do you think we really have a solid grasp of what the human brain is capable? Do you believe we have even begun to understand the nature of our reality? We know very little and have not even begun. How can we remain ignorant to our paranormal reality?

Try as we may through quests, religion and all that comes within, the mystery evades us at each turn. Within us, something says we are more than we seem. Despite this feeling, so many of us continue to deny it. Why? Is it so hard to believe? The proof lies in others who have come before us.

There was a purpose for these beings and there is a purpose for your awakening.

TO BE HERE YOU MUST SLEEP AND FORGET

There are beings that have existed for a long, long, time whose purpose is to help the world. Yes, a part of us might shy away at the childlike simplicity of this. Yet, we do not have to look back far in history to see the truth of what I am saying.

There are glimpses of these old, powerful teachers recorded in our past. Glimpses of beings who changed the course of the world for a greater good.

History records only the ones who stood out, but there have been many. Call them masters or enlightened beings, they have many names but their purposes are similar. Every culture from every period records fragments of stories. These beings were sent to the world, at their time, to stand out. They were sent to make the fabric or the matrix of the spiritual element of our reality stronger. The matrix of spiritual energy vibrates on a higher tonal and is created by the collective consciousness of human beings. Our collective intelligence needed to be seeded and made a little stronger so it would not be weakened by a virus wiping out white cells, making the body of Gaia vulnerable.

These beings have been at certain places around the world and evolved to manipulate a handful so that handful would go out and manipulate a hundred fold and that hundred-fold a thousand-fold. This is how they have managed to get the planet where it is. The human race should have been wiped out already seven, eight, nine times. We are beginning to discover this through archaeology. In fact, there have been times when the human race has almost been completely wiped out but somehow it survived and we do not know how.

How did we do it, our human race?

If we think about it, can human beings run faster than most animals? No. Do we have claws and teeth to defend ourselves?

No. Do we have any great advantage of scent or hearing? The answer is still no. Maybe psychically, we had an advantage, but that is my point. Something intervened, to allow us to make it to this point.

The Universe has always sent beings to assist the world.

Try not to make a complete fairy tale out of this. It is not as if one being comes down and makes the whole world shine and hum with incredible light. It does not work that way. It is about subtleness. It is about the Force working powerfully through our level of reality and then slipping out. It is helping through a steady guided progression without the world ever being fully aware of the intervention. If there was too much progression or things changed too fast it would create an intense backlash, or reaction, from the Darkside. Remember the quicksand, if God struggles too quickly, what happens? It sinks under faster. It must be slow and flexible with a fluidic grace.

The Universe, much like our body system when it senses an illness or an infection, calls upon its white cells.

Where do white cells come from? Our body creates them. How do those white cells know what a virus is from what is not? How is it that a white cell can fight a cold, die, and yet win the battle because the other white cells remember a specific virus so it can never come back again? Even when a white cell dies, a part of it lives.

For a human white cell, memories and essence are stored in their dimensional consciousness. Our white cells have chosen to serve our body just as we must choose to serve the Force. We can tell what is a 'virus' from what is not by utilizing a higher sensory, our sixth sense.

The Darkside changes and evolves just as the Force evolves and grows over hundreds of thousands of years. The Darkside knows what has been going on. As life on this planet swells, it reacts and pushes us back. It wants to prevent life.

This is the best we have done so far. You may have to simply trust me on that.

The Darkside knows about enlightened beings and anticipates them. As the Universe sent enlightened beings, the Darkside began destroying them instantly. It has become a problem for the Universe to send white cells to the Earth to inhabit a body. Yet, they must arrive to do the work, and fulfill their necessary role.

We have gotten so far now, more than any other time in history. Another hundred years and we will easily be pollinating the Moon, Mars and beyond! We will be spreading life throughout the Universe.

The Darkside prevents powerful white cells from inhabiting a body on Earth. It destroys them by preventing them from emerging, by even being born. It blocks them on an energy level. There have been immense conflicts, or exchanges of energy, to stop white cells from arriving on this planet.

The reality of this ongoing conflict is complicated.

The explanation I am about to offer is intentionally simple. Understand that this explanation only examines the basics of a conflict that determines the fate of this planet. There is an amount of God in the universe and there is an amount of the Darkside in the universe. In this dimension, the Darkside has a very strong hold. In some cases, it is more powerful than the Force in this dimension. This is not true for all dimensions, rest assured. Remember that there are higher dimensions where only the Force is present.

In order to prevent the Darkside from blocking White Cells the Universe began delivering them to this world in a state that acted much like a stealth mode.

Because consciousness is a vibration, the Darkside easily detects any high frequency consciousness that moves into this dimension. For it to avoid detection and destruction by the Darkside, a hyper-dimensional consciousness, which is near the tonal of the Force, must enter this dimension as a consciousness with a low tonal.

When a white cell moves into this dimension it cannot take its accumulated knowledge, lest the Darkside detect it. It would easily sense a white cell moving into this dimension, like a glowing neon fish swimming through the deepest, darkest parts of the ocean. This is why white cells must leave their higher consciousness behind. They must become a lower tonal to enter this world. This is why the Sleeper is necessary.

A white cell cannot enter this world with the awareness of what they are. It has to be this way.

The game, that we must win, is to not only move into this dimension undetected, but also to awaken, and then reach enlightenment. Once we reach enlightenment all that we could not move across before, all that we could not bring with us is here, now.

The trial of the Sleeper is to forget all we once were and struggle to awaken.

NOW RISE AND REMEMBER

I have come, I have awakened and reached enlightenment, which is how I know everything we are discussing in this book. However, like any Sleeper, I had to forget everything, lest the Darkside sense me, and had to go through many trials and tribulations before I awoke. Now that I am across, so to speak, and have set up my satellite dish undetected, all of a sudden, I am downloading the Force into this dimension.

Like all those who served the Force before me, I too know I have a responsibility for making the way easier for those who come after.

By figuring out how to awaken, I am able to share and show others who come across. I am here to help you set up the satellite dish, tell you where to direct your dish, or consciousness, to receive the best signal and then wait for the moment when you finally connect and the information comes down.

Then, suddenly, you become Enlightened and my purpose has been fulfilled.

When that happens I have served the Force and done what it needed me to do. That is all I hope for and all I want. This book is to help you find your way to awakening. It is about you choosing to connect to God, so that it can work through you.

I have tried to explain these concepts in the simplest terms possible. Call my explanations cartoonish, call them movie-like. I could go into detail but most would not understand the main point. If I keep the concepts simple, everyone can understand the goal.

We do not remember everything that we are because we could not.

We must struggle through the process of awakening because that is the only way it can happen. We had to fall asleep so that we could silently pass to this dimension, into this world. We have to wake in a world that may seem like a dream, because a part of us feels strongly that there is more. And there is.

Although we had to fall asleep to arrive here safely, our destiny is not to remain asleep.

We are not meant to be here only to experience, that is why we struggle against this veil we feel has been placed over our sight. Remember, even though our purpose is to awaken, there is no guarantee that it will happen. We must choose to actively seek awakening and time is not on our side.

The only guarantee we have in life is that we will have a physical death. Each person has a limited amount of time to experience this amazing and beautiful world.

We have an opportunity to awaken and move beyond the limits of this reality if we so choose and earnestly apply ourselves to this path. If we choose this path, we have a diminishing amount of time to awaken. When we come to this realization, each of us must decide what level of dedication we will give to ensure our awakening before our physical expiration.

I am not a gambler, therefore I have taken the stance that there is never enough time. I have devoted my life to the immediate path of awakening and resolving any and all barriers of resistance in order to help others awaken.

There is a purpose for your awakening and I believe it can and will occur – if you apply yourself.

The best way to achieve this is to have as broad an understanding of the paranormal as possible and develop the sixth sense. This knowledge will help you approach and interpret that which you currently cannot even recognize. I often suggest that people should reflect on their own path. Reflect on how long it took to intellectually get to where you are now. What was it that opened the door to this hidden path for you? When was the moment you realized there was something more beyond this physical life? What did it mean to you at that moment? How much more do you want to know?

Everything that you have read in this book will advance you years beyond what you could discover on your own. I design everything that I create to accelerate your awakening. Why am I doing this? People still believe developing paranormal abilities is the wrong path. As long as this attitude prevails, we are in serious trouble.

More importantly, you have a destination and I believe you must awaken to reach it. It is important to me that you do.

The sixth sense is the crucial ingredient and the missing link to awakening. We can meditate and study books about how we are not our physical bodies. We can learn about energies beyond what our eyes can see. We only acquire true understanding of the paranormal through experience. We need to see auras, visible halo-like light radiating from people. We need to step out from our bodies and move around. How do you think that would alter and accelerate how you understand your true spiritual nature? I can describe what it is like to eat an orange but until a person actually tastes one that individual will not really know what the experience is!

It is not enough to sit and talk about how the universe works.

If you were going on a trip to the Amazon jungle, who would you rather speak with before leaving, someone who read a book about what it was like, or someone who went into the jungle and fought the heat and experienced what life there was like? Of course, you would want to speak to someone who had first-hand experience.

Experience is the greatest teacher and any you can gain is invaluable.

How much more do you think you would learn by going to the Amazon yourself? Any second-hand experience is a poor substitute for the real thing. If a picture is worth a thousand words what is an experience worth?

You must pursue opening your psychic senses because it will allow greater and greater experiences which will increase your understanding of things a thousand-fold. Things to encourage your way line the path in the form of many amazing and mysterious experiences.

Remember our story about following the salmon up the stream to the source? In our tale we needed encouragement to continue following the stream and listen to our instinct, the Navigator, and this would come in the form of crystal coves and other amazing sights.

Our path to awakening is no different.

The Universe will show you many fantastic things along your way. How you experience life and your enjoyment of it will intensify incredibly. Once someone enters into awareness, it is difficult to imagine life without it. There are a variety of ways to create an awakened awareness and open psychic sensory but it is not a simple conversation.

One cannot do without the staple activity of proper meditation. There are many forms of meditation and I have found that many are redundant or do little good, especially in an age of short attention spans. I created my own system of meditation after examining my own awakening and noticing what other systems lacked.

Now let us discuss the importance of this practice and how it affects our multi-dimensional being.

CHAPTER NINE

MULTI-DIMENSIONAL
MEDITATION

MULTI-DIMENSIONAL MEDITATION

Then, without seemingly knowing, you want, and need to become one with IT.

Now you must try to move beyond a simple understanding of the concepts contained in this book. It is not enough to simply know what you have read as if it were nothing but plain information.

To really get it you must experience it.

The greatest breakthroughs on the way to awakening do not come from just talking or reading about it. How would you know what to do with the knowledge if it is not real for you? The best way to become what you seek is for me to show you how to experience it on your own. My specialized meditation technique enhances your sixth sense and plugs you into a multi-dimensional state of consciousness.

This technique differs from methods of meditation that focus only on the body and the brain. Through this practice, a person gains relaxation, stress relief, improved concentration, a greater sense of well-being and a host of other physical, and mental, benefits. However, traditional meditation fails to provide the final step that bridges the brain with the dimensional mind. This final step is our direct connection to life, the Universe, God and who we truly are!

It is why most people begin to meditate and it is the last thing most meditation methods offer.

RE-IGNITING THE SIXTH SENSE

Almost all forms of meditation, from traditional techniques to modern meditation technology, neglect the sixth sense.

As we have discussed, the sixth sense is vital. You cannot completely awaken without it. My system of meditation activates and heightens the sixth sense and connects you to your dimensional consciousness. When that happens you will find everything you are looking for but probably never expected to find.

You will feel utterly complete.

When you use your sixth sense to tap into your dimensional consciousness things once considered impossible, or beyond your perception, will become as real as this book in your hand. Everything in this book you will know to be true, beyond a mere intellectual understanding. Through refinement, study, and practice of my meditation technique your sixth sense will connect you to your dimensional consciousness.

Once the sixth sense is active, one can achieve amazing things.

For now, do not be concerned with those amazing things. In the early stages of development, it is important not to focus on psychic parlor tricks and paranormal abilities. Direct your attention toward using the sixth sense as a tool of communication. I will explain why later.

All other paranormal matters are simple byproducts of achieving your inner awakening. Trust me, once you apply even a little effort things will change very quickly.

Through the meditation system I created, you can reawaken the region of the brain in which the sixth sense resides. In so doing you can reconnect with the Universe and experience it with your modern mind.

The Universe is capable of intellectual processes far beyond our understanding. How and when it chooses to manipulate life is not a simple process for us to understand. It manifests itself through our reality in subtle ways but also through a different perception of time. An incredibly long period of time for us is a very short period for the planet or the Universe.

Evolution is the manifestation of the will of the Universe.

Remember our discussion about the owl, the bird and the butterfly? That relationship is the will of the Force working in this dimension. If the Force functions on so many subtle levels, we should ask ourselves, what else does it influence?

Since evolution is the will of the Universe then evolution has not mistakenly forgotten the sixth sense.

Evolution awaits the re-emergence of this sense within humanity so that humans might re-unite themselves with the Force. Do you think the human race is ready? Are you ready?

THE PURPOSE OF TRUE MEDITATION

Typically, most forms of meditation are practiced by sitting, with the eyes closed. We shut off our sight. We do not move, so we are not really touching anything other than what we are sitting on. During meditation, we attempt to shut off all of our five senses. Because our bodies are designed to collect data they will automatically try to continue gathering information through any available sensory. If the body cannot get anything from our standard five, it will try to push the sixth sense forward. This process is the basis for most meditation methods.

The chances of activating the sixth sense in this way are incredibly remote. It is based on a shameful lack of understanding.

This is why other methods discourage development of the very sense they are unknowingly trying to bring forward. They are simply unaware of the process. Shut off your senses, sit long enough, and hope that the sixth sense, or 'spiritual awareness', will spark. This is how other systems expect you to awaken. It is a prescription for frustration and ultimately failure.

For me this is like playing the lottery.

Using other systems, every time you sit down to meditate there is a one in a million chance your sixth sense might just randomly step forward. For most people, when this happens it triggers an amazing, profound and truly paranormal experience. Of course, there is one problem. Once it happens and you have the experience, how do you get back there? You stumbled across it in the first place by blind luck!

Before I explain why it would be important to go back there, or even seek paranormal experiences, let me restate that you should not concern yourself with paranormal events or abilities, in the very beginning. Rather, concentrate on the sixth sense as a tool of communication.

One is sure to ask what the sixth sense needs to communicate. Every sense we have interprets data from this dimension into experiences. They translate experiences and communicate them to us. We are on a spiritual path seeking our higher consciousnesses and God. How will we find and understand these things?

Will our higher consciousness suddenly appear before us in a flash of light and just say, "Oh, there you are. Hi, my name is Charlie.

Say we need to talk, there are a lot of things about us you don't know and have forgotten." It is an absurd thought. What about God? When the moment arrives for us to connect with the Universe, do we expect the clouds to part, a giant face appearing in the sky, saying, "Oh, there you are. Hi, my name is, well, God. Say we need to talk, there are a lot of things about us you don't know and have forgotten." Then we get to sit, stare up at the clouds, and chat with God as if it were just our next-door neighbor? Equally absurd!

If we did not have words, how would we communicate?

What if there was no written language? We would still have feelings. Emotion is the closest thing to frequency or vibration that we can communicate to the Universe with. We can look at a dog and know what it is without saying 'dog' in our head. If we look at a dog and we look at a spoon, we know through internal feelings or sensations, they are different things. It is very subtle but it is like a separate physical sensation. It is not just that they look different but they also feel different. I do not mean they feel different by touch, I mean internally we register a different sensation when we compare the two.

Our sixth sense delivers that data to us.

It is the sensory that is closest to what we are looking for - a frequency or energy. The more we can learn and understand its language the more we can translate and find our awakening.

Using the sixth sense we can interpret and communicate, without words, the language of the Force.

More than understanding the Force, if you wish to accomplish psychic or spiritual feats you must also think without words. If, for example, you want to do something extraordinary, like float an apple across a room using your mind, how do you think you will do that? Do you think you will just tell the apple, "Hey apple! I command you to float across the room!"? No. Floating an object through the air may seem like an extreme example but it illustrates how amazing a true spiritual breakthrough can be when you achieve it. Without words, you can do it.

Notice I said without words, not without thought.

This is something that is easy to say but difficult to do. As an example, read what I am about to explain and then try it, before you continue reading. First, look around where you are right now and take in every detail. Once you have done that, take a deep breath in and exhale. This last part is going to be really easy. Close your eyes and have total non-thought. Just have complete silence in your brain. Do not allow pictures or songs to flicker through your head. You control your brain so just shut it down and do not think about anything at all.

Sit that way for about a minute before opening your eyes and continuing to read.

After doing this for about a minute you will probably notice, your brain is chattering away, despite any attempts to quiet it. It is busy trying to analyze everything and communicate what it is experiencing. I call this the Babbler. Our brains run their own show whether we want them to or not.

We should not need our brains to explain this very simple experience for us. We should be able to sit quietly and enjoy a moment of silence without thinking at all! It is not a difficult task, so what is there to think about? See how long you can sit and not have words in your head. Songs or sounds count. You will want to have total and complete silence.

It is extremely difficult to do.

The brain always, always, always comes up with something to think about. If you do not let it think in words chances are it will start flashing images or pictures to distract you.

Here is another quick example. Do the same thing you did before, close your eyes and take a deep breath. This time take your right hand and slightly pinch your left forearm, which is the bit of your arm just above your wrist. It only needs to be a light pinch, only enough to feel it, and should not be painful. Focus on the physical feeling of the pinch. Do not think about anything. Pay attention to the physical sensation created by having your skin pinched slightly.

Sit and focus for about the same amount of time, which should have been almost a minute.

After you try, open your eyes and keep reading. If you did it, you probably noticed it was a lot easier to do without thinking than just sitting, trying to maintain silence.

Our sixth sense is severely limited when we do not have control of our brains. Our brains always babble, and unless we quiet them, we will never be able to understand the language of the Universe. The language of the Universe is beyond everyday language.

The last example was to show you a quick way to cheat your way into not having any words in your head. Not having any words in your head is only part of it. It does not mean you will not have thought. A big part of what you gain, using my meditation method, is learning to think differently.

Most people believe that when they are meditating they are trying to perfect complete and total non-thought. There must be absolute silence they think. The people who teach or sell these meditations systems believe this too. This is what all of those ancient yogis talk about, right? Wrong. When those ancient yogis said you must have non-thought, they meant non-words. They meant we must learn to think differently, using a process without words, not without thought.

We still want to think, but in a way so alien to normal thought, we might as well call it something completely different.

It is more of a way to think in energy. I understood this early in my childhood, so my meditation system focuses on the sixth sense as a means to think beyond the limitations of language and structural thinking.

As you work with meditation, the way you experience life becomes clearer.

Over time, you begin to see life with qualities of energy and vibration. Beyond simply seeing, soon you will begin to understand that there is something beyond it all. As you continue to apply the techniques, you will feel the presence of the Universe all around you. This is not as abstract as it sounds. It becomes a very clear, very real experience.

Often you first observe it in nature and general life. When you hear music, birds, or a friend's voice, it is as if these sounds are beautiful music, playing in your head, singing through your being. As your sixth sense becomes more active, it enhances your other senses and increases your awareness.

This sounds simple but it changes every moment of your life. Everything you experience becomes fuller, richer.

Imagine doing something you enjoy, like taking a walk through a local park. You feel a warm breeze on your cheek and hear echoes of laughter in the distance. The sun is shining and you capture something in the experience that gives you a sense of peace. It is a simple moment but a pleasurable one.

Now think, what would it be like if I said that simple experience, without the increased awareness of the sixth sense, is like watching it on television? While you may not realize it, the experience, in comparison, is flat, detached, and not as real as it can be.

FUELING YOUR DIMENSIONAL CONSCIOUSNESS

Practicing meditation and activating the sixth sense enhances our connection to everything. You become aware that the energy of the Universe is within all things. There is a difference between understanding this principle and being able to experience it. Your meditations also tune you to a better frequency. Life becomes more rewarding and fulfilling. You understand life more deeply and become one with it. This happens because of the second thing my meditation technique does. It raises your consciousness and tonal by gathering prana into you.

Awakening and experiencing multi-dimensional consciousness requires fuel.

t requires prana. Prana is the all-pervading vital energy of the Universe. It is the energy that makes up everything and is everywhere. I sometimes refer to it as prana rather than energy. This distinction makes it clear that I am talking about an all-pervading vital energy, not a form of electricity.

Prana is important because everything needs an exchange of energy.

A car does not run without gasoline, a tree does not grow without water and fire does not burn without air. Everything in our universe requires an exchange of energy. Our soul, our consciousness, our dimensional being is composed of and feeds on prana. When I talk about raising tonal, or shifting consciousness to a higher vibration, that requires fuel, it requires prana.

We cannot achieve anything psychic or spiritual without prana.

People, often called psychics, who display paranormal abilities, will say they feel drained after performing paranormal feats. It is very tiring. These acts take a certain kind of fuel and that is prana. We must have fuel to raise the vibration of consciousness, shift into other dimensions and ultimately to awaken.

We cannot awaken without gas to get there.

My meditation technique shows someone how to draw in this energy intensely. It is too detailed to discuss now, as it would take up another book just to explain how it works. If you are not using my system, I strongly urge you to look into it.

We draw prana to us by being aware of it. By simply meditating, using a system designed to do it properly; we can collect and consume prana.

Prana is the fuel that will drive us to awakening. It is the breath of life connecting our dimensional consciousness to our present one.

When we consume enough, we can do amazing paranormal things, things that I probably should not write down. These paranormal feats are achieved when our consciousness is at the proper tonal and one is able to understand them. This is why I frequently urge the pursuit of paranormal abilities. The drive to achieve them will activate the sixth sense, which will enable a bridge to the dimensional consciousness and ultimately accelerate awakening. It is all connected.

The process of awakening requires two primary ingredients, first we must maintain a state of consciousness that uses our sixth sense, and second we need prana. Both aspects are the core of my meditation technique.

One must also have the right intent and understanding. This book will help with that understanding. It will better direct the intent of everything behind meditation. This book will narrow your focus on why you need to awaken. It will correct a common misunderstanding about the sixth sense and mystical experiences.

It is not enough to go out and do any old meditation, as there are so many different kinds. Many people who dedicate their whole lives to meditation have only mastered their brain and body, never even beginning to bridge into the spiritual. Most have never found the missing link.

This is one of the reasons why so many people get frustrated with meditation. We have ignored the importance of the sixth sense and the pursuit of metaphysical experiences. If only they had a key to activate their sixth sense, they would see the payoff for their time spent meditating!

Spending time meditating without developing the sixth sense is like building a space shuttle in your front yard and only thinking it is a picnic table. Can you imagine if someone came over and said, 'You know what you could do with this...' and then showed you how to fire up the engines and blast off into space!

Meditating without a system to activate the sixth sense is like a nice, calm, relaxing picnic table. You have no idea what you can really do with it.

BEYOND THE BRAIN

When I mention the space shuttle, it may lead many people to wonder about meditation technology. Tools that promise awakening or spiritual improvement, light and sound machines, binaural technology, or anything that simulates the physical processes that occur during meditation can be worthwhile in the beginning.

When someone meditates, it is common for their two brain hemispheres, the left and the right, to synchronize. They also begin to relax and enter slower brainwave states such as those normally entered when we are deep in thought, studying or dreaming. There are many other beneficial physical responses to meditation, which we will not discuss here. Available meditation technology is only effective for triggering some of the physical responses from the body. Beyond that, their use is limited.

Until we direct our consciousness to awaken, we will be dependent upon our five mundane senses to interpret experiences.

The reason most people find it difficult to direct the consciousness toward awakening is that they have no idea what that is. It is true that we know we are looking for something. If we only had, at least, an idea of what it is, we would probably find it a lot faster! When we use technology we may feel less stress, improved memory and other benefits, gained from the physical responses to meditation, all of which are good. How will we move beyond that and into something more? No matter how stimulated our brains become we must have a direction to discover what we are looking for.

Technology can only stimulate or aid our five senses because it works on a physical level.

By itself, any technology cannot give us that final missing piece that will lead to awakening. In fact, technology was the very thing that separated us from using our sixth sense abilities to begin with. It will never enable you to move beyond the physical brain. However, technology can aid and support the changes needed in the brain and body to experience amazing breakthroughs. It just cannot do it by itself.

The brain holds us back from being dimensionally open and having spiritual experiences.

Our first challenge then, is to overcome the barriers within our own brain. Once we do this, we must also master a specific state of mind, a fluidic consciousness. That is what prevents us from affecting the Matrix or the collective grid of reality and that is what I help people with. It is not a thing, it is not a sentence, and it is not a word. It is a place of existing and a means of operating from that place. Think about what I just said.

It is a place of existing and a means of operating from that place.

It is a place of consciousness and it is dimensional. All of the miracles from Buddha to Milarepa originate from this place, this state of mind, this consciousness. My meditation will help you discover this along with many other things. It will bind body, brain and soul together. It will allow you to harmonize and allow your dimensional consciousness to work through you.

To make that bridge, and I cannot stress this enough, you must have energy or prana and gaining prana requires awareness.

If you are not aware of prana, how can you ever get it? Once you become aware of something only then can you find it. Water tastes like water until you think about tasting the subtle differences in waters. Then their differences become very distinct. If you are not thinking about it or it is not part of your awareness you simply drink it and swallow it and it does not occur to you that there is a flavor, unless it is strong. You create a certain sensitivity, to find what you are looking for.

Meditation will give you that sensitivity.

My meditation system will magnify that sensitivity far beyond normal as it heightens the sixth sense. It teaches you to notice subtle things. It allows you to distill these very fine sensations. It allows you to collect energy, thereby raising your vibration. My system disciplines your brain, so that it can properly bridge to your dimensional mind.

If you do not discipline the brain, it quickly takes control again, even after a profound realization. Anyone who has ever tried any kind of meditation knows this and everybody forgets this. For that reason one must be consistent with their practice.

Consistent meditation will also make you feel very positive and very happy.

People tell me the best moments they experience and the best days of their lives are when they are meditating regularly and they are immersed in life, not trapped in some isolated monastery. But, the current of the collective consciousness, which is the vibration of the planet, pushes against them and like a tuning fork starts moving their vibration back down to its level and they forget to meditate. Then they completely blow it off, forget all about it, and never remember that they are happiest when they are meditating.

The Earth's tonal is constantly pushing against you, as you exist within Gaia, and that bombardment of tonal will always bring you down to its frequency. At which time you forget what it is to be spiritual. You lose touch with your spirituality. Rather than remain at a higher spiritual level, the affairs of the world consume you. The worst part is you will not even know what happened to you. You will wander and forget you ever felt a purpose.

We are urging humanity toward a higher evolution. We are trying to move humanity forward and ensure the preservation of life.

However, the world is constantly trying to conform you. This is why you must meditate, meditate, and meditate. It is the best way to maintain your tonal.

As your tonal lowers, you will not remember or think of meditating. Everything you have read in this book will slip from your mind and you will only vaguely recall some of what you read. Time is against you. It washes away the ties to your Navigator. It takes this knowledge from you, whereas meditating helps to keep it. It helps to keep you aware and rouse you from sleep.

MULTI-DIMENSIONAL BEINGS

Meditation helps us remain at a higher awareness but we must exercise and reflect on the things we know. One of the greatest things to keep in mind is that we exist in the likeness of God. Everything of biological structure goes smaller, smaller and smaller.

By understanding this, we see that the Body of God is universes, stars, and planets. We see that the Earth is a living organism, which we call Gaia, with all its micro life. We have a micro-universe of organisms living inside of us.

God is multi-dimensional. It is energy that permeates this universe.

The meditation that I created allows us to experience Multi-Dimensional Consciousness. Whenever I tell someone this, they almost always nod their head in understanding. But do they really know? Do you know what that really means?

If we exist in the image of God, we are also multi-dimensional. Where are you right now? We have touched on this idea before. Go ahead and think about it until you can remember or come up with an answer. Perhaps you point to your body, or more specifically maybe to your head, even more specifically you might point to that thing inside your head that is your brain. In truth, we are in three places and meditation works on them all.

This has to become second nature to you. You cannot allow yourself to forget this.

This is knowledge that you are not supposed to know. This is what I call high knowledge. High knowledge is knowledge, of which you are not supposed to be aware. You are not supposed to comprehend this. By understanding this, you can now bridge to extreme levels. By not knowing this, you are limited. It is another control of the governor on your mind.

Are you beginning to fathom the intensity of this? For me I sit back and consider that I exist in three places at once and that moves me. It is extraordinary! We are multi-dimensional beings.

We exist in three places at the same time, all of the time!

The first place in which we exist is this physical dimension. We have a body that collects data, feels, and processes. This body exists in this space. Look around, notice objects or a person that might be nearby. You exist in this first place. Now the next dimension is your inner dimension. This dimension is a part of you. We are not fully aware of this dimension but it affects our being and on some level each of us relate to it. This micro-universe inside of you is an inner dimension that you cannot feel or touch but it is there. You are a part of it.

Now where are *you* right now?

Your body is in the place where you are sitting right now. But, where are you? Point to where you are. Where do you think? Where is your mind?

If I could mark, with a pen, where you feel the source of your consciousness would it be on your scalp? Is the source inside your head, if so where inside? If we opened up your skull, what would we find? Your brain is a machine. It operates on chemicals. It operates on various sequences.

Why is it that you cannot exactly identify where you are?

I would say that you are operating not from the first dimension, meaning in this room or place where you are reading this book. Not the second, meaning the brain and the biological chemicals, but from a third place. A place beyond what our limited physical experience allows us to imagine.

We need to be able to discern who we are.

If you cannot discern who you are then it is very likely you are not the person sitting down reading this book. You are not supposed to be able to comprehend what I am saying. It is supposed to be very confusing, but if you can grasp enough of my message and be aware of it, you will have received part of your freedom. You will have begun to slip past the governor regulating you, because it only controls the part of you that exists in this dimension.

You are a multi-dimensional being who exists in different places at one time.

Remember I said earlier that all of your cells give a consciousness to you. They do not keep this information to themselves. Whatever they experience, you experience. Maybe not completely in the same way, but eventually that data becomes you. If you burn a part of your body, you feel it so you believe you are burning.

Really, it is the cells that are burning, not you.

The information is going from the affected cells to a higher place. The cells are sharing this information with you. The cell understands the information, the organism knows the information, and it gives you a carbon copy of it.

We are all cells giving to the consciousness of the planet.

That is what the next higher being is. We are all part of one organism. The only thing that makes us different is self-realization. To realize you need awareness. You need to quiet the body and still the brain. When the body and brain are quiet, with the proper technique, you can use your awareness to seek out experience, which will bring the third forward, your dimensional consciousness. Once the dimensional consciousness is active, you will also be aware of your body and brain. You can become aware of all three aspects of yourself and move that awareness into higher and lower dimensions. This experience is multi-dimensional consciousness!

Multi-dimensional consciousness is the act of moving three kinds of awareness into a singular consciousness.

Right now, you simultaneously exist in three places but are

probably not aware of them all. In order to bridge your consciousness over to your dimensional consciousness you must gain control of the first two.

Do this by practicing meditation.

You must shift your present consciousness into higher vibrations. It must match the vibration of your dimensional consciousness. Your dimensional consciousness is who you really are. It is the part of you that is waiting to Awaken! It is the part of you that yearns to meditate because it knows that meditating will help you reunite with it.

The meditation you practice must offer a bridge to your dimensional consciousness and not limit its focus to just your brain and body! Do you see the way this works? Do you understand that each aspect of your consciousness must give itself to your will and connect to the next? You can be aware of multiple dimensions at once. If this has not quite sunk in yet go back and read it again. It is highly worthwhile to make the effort and try to understand some of this concept.

CHOOSE TO BECOME

Meditation offers you reflection. It creates and refines your soul. As you gather energy, you give strength to your energy body. We are evolving now, beyond our ancestors. We are thinking more than they thought. We are creating more than they created. We are more than they were. The average education and maturity of a fifth grader could be comparable to the maturity of someone twice their age a thousand years ago.

We are living in a much higher evolutionary state.

The human body is creating and forging a true soul, not just a vision. Our concept of the soul has evolved through churches, religions, and philosophies. Now we desire to create a true soul. With only that desire the body gathers and shapes more energy, so that it will not die. It will move into another body, its next evolution.

If you meditate enough, you will begin to 'get it' and the data that you receive will hit explosive levels that will leave you in awe. It is very common to see flashes and streams of imagery, which is a massive amount of information being downloaded to your brain. However, it takes time and practice to learn how to tap your brain for this information. It is like the global-consciousness Internet and it is there, it is online.

You must let it flow inside of you with a fluidic consciousness. More than willing it to flow, you should let it become you. Let it solidify. Want nothing and allow it to become part of you. It is tricky to understand and do. Try to understand multi-dimensional consciousness and exercise it through proper meditation.

You must choose to become.

You have to let things become you. A plant does not think about the process of its job, it becomes. A tree becomes. Animals do not think about what they have to do, they become. You see, the only thing that does not listen to this law is humanity.

Human beings constantly try to fight their nature. They have forgotten simply how to 'be'.

It is like praying. People who pray tend to only talk at God. Yappity, yappity, yap…what I want, what I want you to do, what I need, what's going on, what Sally needs, what Billy needs, you need to heal them, you need to do this… and it goes on and on.

When you meditate, you listen to God.

You will be amazed at the things God has to tell and show. You allow the Universe to express itself through your cells, your energy. You allow the universe to transform you into what it wants you to become, by meditating and letting this data in.

You have to choose to let it become you.

The problem is everyone has come to think too much like human beings. Of course, you might laugh and say you think like a human because you are one! To that reply, I suggest one should go back and re-read many chapters of this book.

You are more than the vehicle, more than the brain and must strive to be more than human.

This structured way of thinking has trapped you. For example, let us say there is something you think you need to know so you go out and try to learn it, so you can become what you think you need to become. The Universe does not work that way. It gives you the kind of knowledge you need. It has a plan for you.

You see, the Universe has been telling the world what to do since the beginning of time. God has been telling the world to live as an organism and how to live. The Earth has been telling the organisms that live within it how to live. You tell the organisms in your body how to live and what to do. However, you do not do it willfully. These organisms listen and do well. The fact that you desire this knowledge and that you open your mind to the Universe means that you are collecting data. You are collecting experiences.

Open your mind and suddenly you will see things. Reflect on things and you will receive revelations.

Those revelations become profound experiences and life-altering breakthroughs! You must not let your brain dictate your understanding. You must learn to think in a different way.

Evolution, this is what this whole book is about. It is about creating a soul. Although I say evolution, I mean revolution, because we must choose to transform ourselves.

We, meaning you and me and everyone who feels this connected purpose, must choose to move forward and act. We must strive to understand and become this knowledge, because this knowledge is alive. It is alive! It must grow and procreate but it needs us to choose to act on it.

CHAPTER TEN

AWAKEN

AWAKEN

Do you remember?

Everything you have read in this book is a Mandala, whether you fully understand it now or not. The knowledge will grow and expand inside of you, if you allow it to.

You see the knowledge in this book is electricity. It is living fire.

By discussing these things, it is as if I have given you a TV or a satellite dish. Now, it is up to you to sit down, turn on the TV, and set the programming to collect data and receive information. That is what you have gained by absorbing these basic concepts. Now, when you see something, instead of scratching your head and moving on because you do not get it, you can understand it. That little piece of understanding helps hold your focus long enough to discover something amazing, before your attention flips to the next channel, saying, 'I'm not amused by this'.

Now you can comprehend it and move beyond that barrier.

My job is to help seekers, like you, understand what you are, and how to make sense of it. When you make sense of it, you will feel more complete. The biggest barrier to understanding this knowledge is the translation, because human verbalization is so crude. Do you understand what I am saying?

LIVING KNOWLEDGE

If we sit down and watch a movie for two hours, would we be able to describe the whole movie and everything that happened in it? I am not just talking about every event, but every moment and the motion of those moments; how the actor's expressions made us feel versus what they were saying. It would be very difficult because the data of the experience, living inside of us, is more intense. We would know what we felt and what we got out of the movie, but be unable to recreate that experience for another person. It is extremely difficult to recreate, with words, an experience that comes close to the original personal experience.

The difficulty with communicating the information in this book is that it is not simply information.

This is not just a book of interesting philosophical things for you to sit around and think about. It is alive! This knowledge lives; it is an organic thing! It is a living thing and it will open doors in your mind that are nearly unbelievable! By reading this book and reflecting on its ideas and concepts, you are setting up the receiving equipment and learning to download the data. It is beginning. As you read, different parts of you start to put the pieces together, somewhere in the back of your mind.

Your brain starts to crack the code.

Then you begin to feel 'IT'. This triggers a chain reaction, which becomes something completely more than only the culmination of this information. It flips a switch and you begin to really experience things.

The only way for you to really understand is after the download of dimensional knowledge begins. There is no way for me to tell you everything that I know. We have no words to describe what I know or how I know it. Yet, words are what I have to give you. I do not give them in hope of simply passing on what I know, but how to know it.

I am offering a map of how to find this knowledge.

That has been my purpose for writing this book, creating my meditation system and all the material I have made. My purpose has been to design a method for you to experience this knowledge for yourself. It has been a process of trying to figure out the best way to give people the necessary equipment, so to speak, to collect the data. It is a difficult process because there is no way, in this body with these muscles, this tongue, and these lungs for me to think of enough words to begin to express all of this information.

However, if you can receive the knowledge, your brain can create a universe. Then you begin to understand and you are on your way to Enlightenment. By reading this book, you are already waking up!

The problem is that you are trying to find a way to crudely understand it in the same way you would understand other basic knowledge. The same way that a person can mathematically come up with an equation, this book teaches you how to equate the universe and how to equate your relationship to it. That does not mean you cannot deviate from this source to get other information. You can. However, the most common obstacle in the journey toward fully realizing this knowledge is in not meditating enough.

The other problem is the brain thinking too much on a structural level. If you can remove that and look at things in a very relaxed way, letting it flow without forcing it, using fluidic consciousness, everything will make sense.

Reflect on what you have read in this book.

Nurture it in the back of your mind until it becomes strong and alive in you. Because you will forget, be forewarned, you will forget if you do not strive to remember. It will happen as a result of the tonal of the planet, the vibration of its consciousness. It is the current of the collective consciousness constantly pounding on you. It is the stream trying to push you back into the ocean.

STRUGGLE TO AWAKEN, SURRENDER TO BECOME

The most amazing thing is that as much as you may want to awaken, as much as you might love to feel that energy, that peace within yourself, and the wonder of that place, you will still forget. This thought alone should be as intense as a UFO hovering right over your house, then landing in your backyard, and having aliens walk out! Think about how strange it would be! It would be completely shocking!

It is no different when we fall asleep in our pursuit to Awaken.

There is something that you have either experienced, that profoundly changed you, or you feel a strong urge to experience, then it vanishes. It evaporates, as if you give a quick snap of your fingers and poof, any desire you have to Awaken is suddenly erased. That alone should make you want to meditate more. That should make you want to Awaken more.

One moment you feel compelled to seek out knowledge, like the kind in this book, and then suddenly the desire vanishes. That desire is a force of energy.

You are struggling to reach a state of mind. You are at war with the tonal of the planet. You are at war with the Darkside. None of it wants you to get ahead. Think back about the story of the salmon. Remember all of the dangers and obstacles it had to face on its journey. There are bears, otters, dams, choices of which stream to take and even the very current of the river it is swimming against!

It is a struggle.

In the beginning, there is the struggle. Life is a struggle when you are born, and it is painful. Only upon death do you finally surrender to real life. There is a struggle that you go through to Awaken. After you struggle you begin to enter awareness. Awareness then is a struggle because it is a flood of knowledge. Then eventually you start sorting it all out and you come to terms with things. It is at that moment that you dedicate yourself.

Then you enter into Enlightenment.

Enlightenment is another struggle. It is a struggle of questioning reality. It is the very extreme realness of it that makes you question it so strongly. You question if it is real and if it is 'IT'. As you enter Enlightenment, I give you this advice.

Do not fight it.

What you do with it is the next problem. That is your next battle. I will tell you now, do not try to conquer the struggle directly because you will lose. Let the struggle run around you, never tackle it, never grasp it, let it be.

I often relate the struggle to awaken as being like a matador fighting a bull. Think of fighting a giant bull. It is twice your size, sheer muscle, with sharp horns that can easily gore you. When it lowers its head and charges you, how will you fight it? Will you attempt to grab it by the horns and wrestle it to the ground? Will you try to use brute force against brute force? Or will you take your cape and just when it strikes, step aside and move away, dancing around its every attempt to bring you down?

If you have ever watched a bull fight, you know that the matador always dances around the bull, never directly engaging it. The bull exerts all of its energy trying to spear you with its horns and yet you surrender, stepping aside at the last moment.

Such is your way to awakening. This is what I mean when I say that you should not try to tackle the struggle directly. The more that you push yourself to understand something that you are not ready for, the less likely you are to achieve understanding! You must surrender, let go and be fluidic.

You cannot force this door to open. It does not work like that.

Typical structured thinking will not gain you entrance to this place. If you want the winds to rise for you, learn to be fluidic. If you want to walk on water, learn to be fluidic. If you want to heal the sick, learn to be fluidic. If you want to see dimensions, open up gateways, and do all of these things, willfully, you must be fluidic. If you demand these things from yourself, or the Universe, you will never have them. They are too heavy. Learn to be fluidic and the power you can tap is limitless. That is the next direction.

THE MOMENT OF CHOICE

The world needs you to Awaken.

It needs you to remember. On every level you could look at it, there is greatness in undertaking the task of awakening. It will transform your life and those whose lives you touch. Your awakening will affect the tonal of the planet, and enhance the feeling and vibration of the whole. How could you forget the feeling of that purpose?

We have discussed how everything is energy and energy works in vibration. The collective pool of experiences and the consciousnesses of everyone on the planet make the consciousness of our world, Gaia. The consciousness of Gaia has a vibration, a tonal. When you meditate, or even just think about prana or the Force your consciousness rises in tonal. The vibration or consciousness of God, the Force, exists at a very high tonal.

After you go through the process of Awakening and finally reach Enlightenment, you will have set up a direct connection to the Force, which allows it to channel through you.

Imagine there are hundreds of thousands of little gray wires floating in empty space. Now imagine that one of these wires starts to hum or vibrate slightly. It makes a sound almost like a ringing or like a song of pure tone. The wire starts to increase its vibration and starts to hum louder and louder. It begins to visibly shake and vibrate. The wires next to it then start to slowly shake or vibrate and hum a lower tune. The original wire that first began vibrating is at the highest note and reaches a vibration of such intensity that it starts to glow like the filament inside a light bulb.

Suddenly it explodes with incredible light.

Soon the other wires around it pick up the higher vibration, similar to idle tuning forks next to a vibrating tuning fork, and the idle forks will increase their vibration. The initial little gray wires begin to faintly glow and the ones next to them slowly begin to vibrate and hum. The result is an exponential growth as the light spreads and increases from one, to ten, to one hundred, to one thousand and on and on until the light is so great, darkness cannot penetrate it.

It all began with a single moment.

That moment was a choice, which began an explosive transformation. The process is evolution, but the choice is a revolution. As you choose to remember your purpose and begin to Awaken, you make it easier for others who follow you.

Your decision affects the vibration of our collective consciousness.

Remember the research done on the little birds that drank milk by pecking through cardboard lids? There is a collective consciousness. The moment when the learned habit of a few birds exploded, into the entire population, is proof of this collective consciousness.

A moment for humanity is coming, when, like a dam giving way, knowledge will flood in. Choose to revolt and fight against that which holds us captive and asleep.

You do not need to march, shout angry slogans, or do anything that most people associate with revolutions. You need to stay awake, and keep your consciousness in a fluidic state. Of course, like all revolutions, it requires a struggle and it requires a choice. In this revolution, you must choose to struggle.

You can forget everything you have read in this book, forget that you ever felt a purpose and forget your need to Awaken. You can simply go back to sleep. You can also choose to push past the system of laws governing this dimension, which control your consciousness, and choose to remember who you really are! Realize the urgent need to Awaken! Realize the nature of this grand cosmic struggle and wake up!

The power is in your hands.

You must choose to serve the Force. Do not wait until the Force comes to you. Much of what you have learned in this book is how truly enormous the Universe and God really are. We are so very tiny in comparison to the big picture. Like a single salmon in comparison to the world. Real growth cannot come until one is truly humbled by just how small they are.

People often want to believe God is focused and aware of them. In doing this they minimize how great and vast God actually is. If we believe God is aware and focused on us then we also end up waiting for God to acknowledge us. We wait for God to choose us.

You must choose to find your way to God rather than wait for God to find you.

Choose to become Aware! You must decide to move into God's awareness and follow that route. Take heart in knowing that if our little salmon, a small micro spec of life, can make it to the source, so can you. By going through that process, even if you are physically by yourself, you have joined us. You have joined those who are struggling through the darkness, to bring the world into light.

There may be times when you question if you are alone, or if there are others in the world that are with you, or if it matters at all. Be assured, there comes a time when you know everything in this book is true, there also comes a moment when you will know you are not alone.

Your struggles give more than most ever know and more than you may possibly conceive at this moment.

There may come a moment when you open your eyes and the world will not be as it was when you closed them. In this moment, you feel and may even 'see' those of us who have been there, all along, walking and struggling with you. You may look ahead and see those who have struggled to pave the way for you, and looking back you may see those who have an easier way because of your struggles.

It is here, in this moment, which will be the longest and shortest you will ever know, you will laugh, that I have futilely tried to explain anything written in this book. You will see the precious fragility of life and realize, if anything, I did not tell you enough and have kept the direness from you. You will realize everything I created had to be done.

During this moment, and ever afterwards, there will be a place in your heart, where you never know loneliness, never know fear, hate or sorrow, and you know that the words love, peace and joy do injustice to what dwells there, within you.

You will be complete.

The future is uncertain and this calling, this purpose, for those of us who feel it inside, is there for a reason. Something far beyond us planted that seed, that purpose, as part of its grand design and direction. It is a hope, this seed, this Navigator, that against the odds, you will make a choice.

What are you waiting for?

The time has come for you to join the r*evolution*.

The time has come for the Sleeper to Awaken.

THE NEXT STEP IS YOURS

Higher Balance Institute is dedicated to giving you all the tools and knowledge you need to empower yourself and transform your life. The purpose and mission of the Institute is to awaken the world one mind at a time. Towards fulfilling that goal we know the greatest results come when you can experience something for yourself rather than just reading about it.

WHAT ARE YOU WAITING FOR?

If you would like to continue your Higher Balance experience, contact us now!

Higher Balance Institute's programs were created with the purpose of stimulating and activating the dormant sixth sense, the missing link to spiritual awakening. The material is suitable for everyone, whether you are a novice or advanced.

Higher Balance material is an at-home system that can be learned easily and comes with everything you need to accomplish your goals. It is the most powerful program on Earth! Join us and the thousands of others worldwide who have experienced the Higher Balance material.

HIGHER BALANCE INSTITUTE

515 NW Saltzman Road #726
Portland, OR 97228
Phone: 800-935-4007
Fax: 503-626-8157
Web: www.higherbalance.com
Email: publishing@higherbalance.com

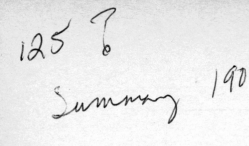

125 ?

Summary 190